Microgreens

Start your own Sustainable Urban Microgreen Farm for profit and pleasure using Vertical Farming techniques for Gardeners in Hydroponics and Soil

By

Millie Marguerite

Particular creators claim all copyrights not held by the distributor.

The data in this is offered for educational purposes exclusively and is all-inclusive as so. The introduction of the data is without a contract or any assurance confirmation.

The marks used shall be without consent, and the distribution of the mark shall be without the consent or support of the proprietor of the mark. All trademarks and trademarks within this book are just for explanation and Are held clearly by the owners, who are not associated with this record.

TABLE OF CONTENTS

INTRODUCTION

When the global human population rises and megacities arise, there is a tremendous need for arable land to fulfill the food market and decrease malnutrition. Conventional farming activities contribute to deforestation of the soil for agricultural crop growth and intensification in order to generate higher yields per unit area. Such practices have been planned to have a detrimental impact on the atmosphere causing contamination of soil and water. In order to produce higher yield per unit of space than traditional outside farming it is necessary to consider the use of vertical farming technology which uses both horizontal and vertical field and efficiently uses nutrients, water and time (off-season produce with artificial lighting). Microgreens have been taken into account in a revolutionary vertical cultivation as they are high in phytonutrients and can be extracted in a limited period. Within this paper we discuss the existing increasing conditions of vertical farming microgreens, such as crop range, media, sun, solution of nutrients and containers and define information gaps. In addition, studies in this field will contribute to improved conditions for addressing global problems and challenges related to food health, protection and utilization of capital.

Microgreens are unique plants, herbs and flowers picked as young as possible, usually at the first true growth point, though at times at the seed leaf level (cotyledon). The vegetables are used as garnishes or scattered around entrances and sweets for gourmet salads. Besides its flexibility and future productivity, the microgreens are nutrient-dense, strong and simply lovely. When grown in a greenhouse with additional heat or under light indoors, micro greens will easily be generated throughout the year, including at high latitudes.

As a consequence of rural to urban transformation megacities are developing because of rising wealth and metropolitan populations. The reduction of the forest to arable land leads to degradation, leading to the depletion of natural resources, such as the usage of groundwater, rising habitats as a consequence of habitat destruction and intensified soil erosion, and greenhouse gas pollution. Around the same period, more fast food than organic diets have been adopted by the metropolitan population, resulting in a growing degree of health problems. A current trend of use of increasingly refined feeds like beef, fruit and vegetables involves improvements in agricultural production processes, in particular the intensification of agricultural production. Agricultural intensification at the field level would contribute therefore to the extensive usage of fertilizers and herbal defense pesticides, which would also raise soil and groundwater contamination.

The production of sustainable agriculture is critical in providing reliable and nutritious food, taking into account food protection and safety, through efficiently managing resources without adversely affecting the climate. Urban communities lack policies, systems and technology to provide rising citizens with nutritious, secure food. Understanding the megacities 'innovative technologies will better navigate our planet's potential. Intensive organic cultivation is another method of sustainable agriculture which involves the deployment of bulk organic feed materials and pest management, which contribute to processing costs and potential degradation of the ecosystem. In this scenario, vertical farming in megacities plays a critical role in providing resource productivity for food and nutrition conservation.

The planting of these crops under specific technologies advanced results in higher development costs due to the need to manage the weather, constant procurement and recirculation of the quality irrigation water and nutrients, and post-harvest handling costs before the commodity hits the user. It will inevitably raise the retail price of the goods that citizens with low wages cannot afford. Thus, the implementation with advanced vertical farming technology is necessary, to reduce manufacturing prices without losing product quality. Microgreens are used as suitable crop since they are rich in phytonutrients and vitamins while the external application of fertilizers is not required. Microgreens are young plants, with strong flavors, bright colors and delicate texture of fruits, herbs and beans. Microgreens are now facing a high price on the market owing to their rich nutrient value and post-harvest activities that low-income consumers can not afford to purchase by introducing them to their daily menus for their wellness. This analysis is concerned with the development of highly nutritious and healthy foods (without microbial contamination) with limited waste after harvest by-production costs utilizing vertical containerized agriculture technologies.

VERTICAL FARMING TECHNOLOGY

The vertical cultivation enables the growth of high value crops with higher yields than that produced through traditional farming by the better usage of resources such as soil, fertilizer, energy and time, and thereby decreased carbon footprint. This technique more efficiently utilizes both horizontal and vertical spaces to achieve greater volume production per unit of temperature, light, carbon dioxide and humidity under regulated environmental conditions. Various kinds of vertical cultivation engineering such as hydroponics, geoponics and aquaponics are used and tracked successfully for physical and chemical criteria such as water content, pH and solubility. Provided that vertical agriculture is practiced in a closed and regulated setting, the sunlight as a light source for photosynthesis is substituted by artificial lights of different range and intensities. In such a situation, high-energy performance and longevity LED lights are more efficient than conventional light sources such as fluorescent lamps.

Hydroponics

Commercial hydroponics is a modern technology which involves nutrient solution plant growth without using soil as a rooting medium. This ensures the inorganic nutrients are added through irrigation water and nutrient recirculation solution to avoid wastage by leaching. The key benefits are the prevention of soil issues such as crop-borne pathogens, weak physical and chemical properties and a lower consumption of plant defense chemicals. Hydroponics contributes to better fruit and flowers with specific fertilizer application. Hydroponics 'drawbacks are higher construction costs, maintenance costs and technical expertise needed to operate them to reach optimum production and reliable goods under managed environmental conditions.

Before Beginning the Urban Farm Business Plan

Before you start designing your business strategy, remember the key reasons for beginning an urban farm. Documenting the motivations to start a company can help you prioritize the business plan and recognize problems, tools and skills required for the business plan to be created. Ultimately, recognize the principles you carry to the company and the principles that are essential for the company 'success.

Consider the following questions:

- • Would you have agriculture or field experience to help you run your field or do you need to protect your skills elsewhere?

- • Would you be interested in crop processing, animal husbandry, aquaculture, aquaponics or non-food products?

- • Do you have a property for your urban farm or are you selecting a place?

- • Are you operating the farm as a non-profit community-based project including community leaders in the operation?

- • Would you grow the farm as a means of income and revenue?

- • Are you establishing the farm as a household company and revenue source?

- • Is there a common skill or commodity you like to market?

- • Would you create a farm for other companies, such as an agency or restaurant, to supply products?

- • Who's going to be part of the organizing team?

- • Do you have the skills to build the business plan's promotion, service, human resources and financial plans or to help launch the company?

- • Do you require skills to cope with environmental issues and clean-ups that could be correlated with an urban property that you intend to grow?

- • Do you require experience in designing plans, performing surveys or organizing development?

- • Would you require money to gain this expertise?

- • Was this farm economically motivated?

- • Do you want to make a benefit, break-even, or do you want a source of charitable income on a farm?

- • Is the farm to rely on the community?

- • To what degree do environmental issues such as organic fertilizers and resource utilization contribute to the operation of the farm?

BASIC EQUIPMENT FOR INDOOR AND OUTDOOR PRODUCTION

The Guidelines presume that the growers, particularly in non-summer months, already have an indoor area or a hoop house or greenhouse available for growing microgreens during their operations. They may be grown on bed tables in shaded areas without a roof, but over the year, they are not sufficient to start selling in a larger scale. The procedure must be carried out in a hoop house or greenhouse system with a certain approximation of temperature regulation and cooling, for example elevating lateral walls or louvered vents.

There are also many systems and equipment that we have defined as necessary or helpful for the success of our microgreen project. Most farmers have or may create such systems from reclaimed or low-cost resources or find other solutions. All of this is covered in the bed construction and media portion.

Heating System: Hoop house would be passively solar powered, which functions very well for plant start-up early in spring, but had to be augmented to deliver a good micro-green crop in cold and low solar months in winter. Research has shown that several solutions exist in order to heat the environment, but that thermal fluid fed heat mats are the most effective direct thermal choice. There are many choices available for heating water, power, coal, solar and biogas.

Elevated growing area: While not completely required, farmers can operate on an elevated table such as the bed framework to grow microgreen seeds and harvest even more efficiently and comfortably than on a functioning ground floor. It is much simpler and productive for farmers to continue with an elevated scheme for the amounts of microgreens produced for commercial selling. It requires a space that is large and usable from either side if the base consists of reclaimed products or qualified rolling tables. The distance of the bed from each usable side will not be broader than the farmer's length.

Heat Mats: This is an ideal way to heat up the rising area without adding power to the whole hoop house, and large-scale, power-circulating mats with a hot fluid are more powerful and cost effective than electric ones. Many farmers might also have many equipment or other ideas for heating the increasing field, which will also help to provide the warmth needed in the winter.

Water: Microgreens need to be kept continuously at optimal humidity levels such that water in the planted region is available. The working watering equipment remained straightforward: the most versatile performers were long hoses with long neck spray dolls that unleash a soft shower flowing through the tables and offering reasonable coverage.

Ventilation: Big fans will ventilate to avoid mushrooms in winter and to keep microgreens cool in summer. We sustain the increasing region at a degree of temperature and humidity that the farmer can manage. They are critical for the success of the through activity. For household box fans, basic fans can be useful for larger barn fans on rolling stands that can be positioned and guided at various speeds when appropriate. Two extra fans are located on the top of the building to ensure adequate air movement.

Processing Area: In order to wash the microgreens and a broad food grade surface table, a sink is needed to dry them.

Packaging: Based on the specifications of the manufacturer, a durable packaging should be taken that breathes to avoid a soggy microgreen and lasts longer after packaging.

Refrigeration: After harvesting and packaging, microgreens must be cooled before shipping. Nevertheless, for this reason a home refrigerator used will fit perfectly.

MATERIALS

You may need a few supplies to start developing microgreens. Many of you are currently on hand:

• **Planting media**, Such as potting or foam sheets or textiles specially made for the processing of microgreens. Note that any compost or soil potting mix can increase the risk of soil-borne illness.

• **Trays** (1020 flats or 20-row seed flats)

• **Something to cover the seeds after sowing** (paper towel, vermiculite, humidity dome, or white plastic tray)

• **Heating mats, circulation fans, and lighting** (for indoor or off-season production)

GROWING TECHNIQUES TO GET BEST HARVEST

SEED SELECTION

The collection of seeds is an important step. It is better to begin with a few different varieties and later diversify or continue with a prepared blend. Johnny's sells mixes that create a variety of colors, tastes and textures at growth rates consistent.

Many varieties can be ready within 2 weeks but this period can be up to 4 weeks, depending on the variety range and the climate. Coordinate seed times to produce the best sized and flavored blend of varieties. Mustard and radish greens, for example, develop more rapidly than beets, chard or carrots. This may require trials so that accurate records are kept.

SITE SELECTION

Because of the delicate existence of the plant, micro greenhouses or other defensive structures are more commonly cultivated. It is necessary to have sufficient temperatures, ventilation and lighting. Growing on raised platforms or tables often prevents bending to tend plants.

SOWING

Growers normally sow seeds in either 1020 regular flats or 20-row seed flats measuring 1–1 1/2 potting centimeters. Break dense seed on the growing medium with 1:8-1:4 "divided seeds and push seeds tightly into the growing medium for optimum interaction with the soil:

• Small seeds: 10–12 seeds per square inch

• Large seeds: 6–8 seeds per square inch

Too dense seeding may contribute to a lack of air circulation and an increased risk of disease. Using a sifter or colander, seeds may be sorted by size and an acceptable seed density calculated. Water-in softly to prevent throwing the seeds clean. Cover seeds throughout the germination process to retain sufficient moisture. Seeds should be protected by soaked sheets, loosely sifted vermiculite, a tiny potting mix, an inverted white bowl, or moisture cap. If you use a tray or cap, take caution in bright, warm weather to remove the cover or ventilate; otherwise, it may be too hot a temperature to avoid germination. They can be kept moist while using towels and can be extracted gently after only a few days. Most seed coats are separated with the cloth, which is beneficial when the finished product is to be cleaned.

SUCCESSIVE SOWINGS

Due to the one-cut existence of this crop, succession planting is needed to provide a constant supply of microgreens. Seeds will be planted dates and amounts dependent on consumer requests, distribution times and person growth levels. All variety availability and environmental factors impact growth rates; we suggest that you maintain comprehensive notes to allow a stronger change to the program.

TEMPERATURE

Ideal temperature of the soil for germination and development depends on the individual need of each species; for instance, the optimum temperature is higher for heat-loving crops such as basil than for colder brassicas. For unique rising statistics for each variation, see the rising details on Johnny's website or collection. However, optimum atmospheric temperatures are usually between 65–75 ° F/18–24 ° C. **Temperatures above 75°F/24C° can inhibit germination in some varieties and increase disease pressure.** Moderate night dips are reasonable but continuous, higher temperatures facilitate the development of maximum speeds.

AIR CIRCULATION

Good circulation of air is essential for disease prevention and healthy development. Be vigilant not to sow too big. Using horizontal airflow fans to maintain a steady airflow in your greenhouse or through area.

WATERING

For good germination, steady moisture is essential. When germinated, microgreen water flats daily, but do not often saturate the newspapers, as this may contribute to disease. Based on the rising method, either top or bottom-water. If you have top watering, a mister, a soft push or a spray bottle may be used. The under watering choices can involve ebb-and-flow tables, floors or structures of hydroponics.

FERTILIZER

The pure water is usually the best for rising media with any fertility, like potting mix. Watering with a diluted fertilizer solution is ideal for products lacking an intrinsic nutrient benefit such as foam or coir pads, or for slow developing plants that may lose nitrogen before harvesting. Once fertilized, add fertilizer into the growing medium before sowing or using a watering device for liquid applications to avoid fertilizer residues from settling on the plants. Taking note to stop "off-aromas," often resulting from fish-based fertilizers.

DISEASES

Thanks to their high density, micro greens may be vulnerable to disturbances such as damping, low air quality and polluted newspapers. Ensuring air ventilation with horizontal ventilators, using safe media and water supplies, using sufficient seeding intensity and not overwater.

TIPS FOR CHALLENGING VARIETIES

There are two things that make some varieties more difficult to grow than others.

1. **Large seed size:** Larger seeds require a longer period to make effective contact with the rising media and must be tightly pushed into the soil and properly protected to hold seeds moist during germination. There's also an urge to seed less when seeds are bigger, particularly in varieties that have multiplied seeds such as cilantro, beets and chard. The thickness of the seed

thus offers sufficient room and can also be planted 1/8-1/4 inch apart.

2. **Slower germinating varieties:** For both over and under watering of varieties are sluggish to germinate, take note that flats are regularly moist (not saturated) and maintain sufficient air ventilation to mitigate disease. Supplementary heat is often helpful in faster germination in varieties that need colder temperatures for successful germination.

OFF-SEASON GROWING

Indoors or in a greenhouse at northern latitudes, growing microgreens during off season may entail additional effort. You may require additional lamps, air fans and probably a heat mats for rising the through medium temperature and/or extra heat for increasing ambient temperatures.

Many plants react differently to artificial light than natural light. Light duration, strength and the distance from the lighting device to the crop decides the finished product growth rate and price. If the light source becomes too small or too far removed from the flower, it may become spread or lame. Crop color can appear washed off if the strength of light is not enough. If the light is too bright, the crop will easily dry out or look burnt.

DAYS TO MATURITY

Since microgreens grow rapidly, plant size and yield amounts will alter dramatically per day. The amount of days of ripening not only ranges, but also relies on the conditions of developing, such as temperature, humidity and sunshine. If you develop outside under covered cover conditions, the number of days to maturity can differ greatly.

HARVEST, PACKAGING, AND STORAGE

Microgreens are typically harvested when first collection of true leaves are produced, with cotyledons still attached, normally between 1 and 2 inches long. The presence and flavor of each variety will give you an idea of the optimum harvest period. Any checking is good. Microgreens may either be sold fresh, or bagged or clams can be sliced and shipped. Selling live goods in trays will save time and improve shelf-life. The common method is to cut micro-green harvests. Microgreens priced by weight are typically clipped as near as possible to the foundation without having the medium in the final product. Split the increasing medium into the perfect size while selling a live commodity.

When live goods are sold, cooling is essential to preserve consistency and freshness after harvest – the shelf-life is 5–10 days under the right conditions.

REFINING AND ADJUSTING YOUR SYSTEM

Since too many factors will influence growth rates and production, we suggest that you check varieties and take thorough notes of growth rates and results with your particular growth scenario. You can note differences between crop types while compiling your results. You can note, for example, that most radishes yield comparable amounts per flat as many of the other brassica varieties. This knowledge may be used to extrapolate between varieties within plant families.

VERTICAL FARMING CONSIDERATION

Crop Selection

The variety of crops will be a significant factor that is strongly affected by suitability, customer desire, competition and the market. High-value commercial crops are tailored to vertical cultivation, which offers strong competition, improved buyer interest and higher rates to cover rising development costs. The cost of output will be decreased by crops with lower irrigation, such as decreased water use with high water usage and reduced nutrient application. Over the last 20 years, there has been tremendous demand for vegetables with strong health benefits. In the new food paradigm and market choice, microgreens, classified as "vegetable confects and specialty crops" retained its value. Micro greens are delicate plants, with an extreme taste and vivid colors and delicate texture of vegetables and herbs and grains.

Therefore, they may be applied to enhance color, texture and flavor in lettuce, soups and sandwiches. It has been documented that microgreens produce higher levels of phytonutrients (ascorbic acid, β-carotene, alphoenol and phylloquinone) and minerals (Ca, Ag, Fe, Mn, Zn, Se and Mo) and lower nitrate content than their mature leaf equivalents to support adult and child diets without exposing them to harmful nitrogen. It is very necessary to select a crop containing high-grade phytonutrients, carotenoids, antioxidants and medicinal properties.

Media Selection

A growth medium is a substance that encourages plant production. A variety of non-toxic porous materials were used to shape the growth substrates of plants such as rockwool, perlite, pumice, extended mud, assorted volcanic rocks, polyurethane foam and coconut coir dust. A balanced distribution of small and larger pores in a substratum is important to ensure sufficient water access to plants without compromising the supply of root oxygen. In regular, loose, sterile germinating media including peat, vermiculite, perlite and cocoon fiber, microgreen can be made. Alternate processing strategy involves the placing of fibers as mat or padding (acting as a seeding bed), on the bottom of a burlap or a food-grade plastic tray crafted specifically by the company "Ready to Build" (Beachwood, OH), for micrograins.

In soil proof communities, peat is widely used as a method to plant microgreens, but in Thailand, peat is transported from Europe and thus is a costly product.

Therefore, the ability of other biomaterials as a replacement for peat was explored to render-media more accessible. The findings indicate that the biomaterial available at the site, such as coconut coir dust, sugarcane filter cake, or vermicompost, is efficient and inexpensive in producing high yield micrograins while retaining a healthy level of Escherichia coli, Staphylococcus aureus, and Salmonellasp. For another trial, Rapini microgreen were developed for contrast to costly and non organic peat and synthetic mats (Sure to Grow company, Beachwood, OH, USA) and were sub-pricely, environmentally safe, biodegradable recycled textile fiber and kenaf fiber. Plants grown under textile fiber and jute were found to have a higher yield with a lower nitrate content than peat and synthetic mats, which is also a strong substitute to peat and synthetic mats.

BioStrate is the latest media for microgreen farming and is widely accessible on the market. But the use of BioStrate as a tool for microgreen cultivation is without literature. BioStrate is a bio-based fiber for the processing of hydroponic microgreens and baby salads. It is a blend of biopolymers and natural fibers engineered to handle applied water effectively for optimum growth (Grow-Tech LLC and the source is green growers). BioStrate is compact and user-friendly. It's compost worthy. There are therefore no literatures on the growth of microgreens under liquid gel medium or semisolid media containing all these important nutrients for microgreen growth and production which prevent further use. BioStrate is therefore a medium for growing a microgreen and its capacity for growing higher yield compared with other biodegradable environmental media is to be evaluated. Murashige-Skoog medium widely used in the cultivation of vegetative tissue may be considered for growth of microgreen.

Light Source

Light is an essential element that the plants use to allow a photosynthesis. Plants grown in this area benefit from Sun. Because plants are grown in regulated environment under vertical farming technology, they need external light sources for their photosynthesis. Conventional sources of light such as high-pressure sodium lamps and metal halide lamps produce high heat and are not energy efficient or cost-effective. Solid-state light-emitting diode (LED) lamps have since been developed to address these problems and to boost product efficiency. Three light criteria, such as strength, temperature and length should be taken into consideration, which have specific impacts on crop growth and product consistency, such as the energy output, low maintenance costs and durability. For photosynthesis, plants need 400 to 700 nm of wavelength of light, called visible light spectrum and photosynthesis active radiation. The plant pigments absorb the blue, green and red-light spectra and have a significant effect on plant growth and production. The high red and infrared light impact germination and flowering but are less absorbed by the seeds.

Nonetheless, each plant species can require a defined spectrum of light, intensity and duration and there is a substantial information gap in the suitability of light spectrum, intensity and duration for microgreen growth.

LED Spectrum

The net photosynthetic levels were found to be higher under the red (650 nm) and blue (440 nm) combinations and lower red and blue (720 nm), when an experiment to establish the influence of LEDs on the net photosynthesis, growth and blue (440 nm) chrysanthemum plantlets was performed in vitrogrown MS medium. Red and far-far far variations of the strongest propensity, however the fragility of the tigers. Shot development outside elongation was the highest under red-blue and fluorescent light combinations. As Lactuca sativa was grown with a particular light range of red curly lettuce, it is observed that the synthesis of anthocyanin, protein and phenylalanine ammonia-lyase enzymes is strongest in combination blue and red light emission. A separate study showed that the growth of microgreens, primarily blue lights showing greater cotylledon region and a higher fresh density, improved chlorophyll a and anthocyanin pigment material, in red and green basil (Ocimumbasilicum) was cultivated with blue and red LED. Stimulation of the phänolic synthesis and free radical scavenging is enhanced by mainly green cultivar light and red cultivar blue light, which reveals that LED light has an effect on the leaf's color.

LED and Photosynthetic Photon Flux Density

In the experiment performed to evaluate the effect in low or high photosynthetic behavior of lettuce leaves of black, Red and blue LED, the biomass and photosynthesis parameters were found to be rising with a light voltage of 238 µmol5-02-1 vs 80 µmol5-02-1 under the blue LED illumination. In another analysis, carried out on the adequacy of light irradiance rates in borage microgreens for the optimum growth of nutrients, it was found that the lowest nitrate contents and the highest antioxidant concentration were reported with moderate irradiance rates of 330-440 µmol5-02-1 and were, therefore, suitable for borage microgreen cultivation.

LEDs and Energy Efficiency

LED agriculture (95% red and 5% blue) requires 50% less energy per unit consumed by dry biomass than conventional light sources, which indicates that substantial energy usage savings is accomplished when utilizing LEDs than conventional sun. An indoor experience with basil and strawberries showed that when handled with LEDs with maximum energy quality than traditional fluorescent lamps and spectral red, the plants expressed enhanced biomass, fruit production, antioxidant and lower nitrate levels: blue 0.7 was necessary for proper plant growth with improved nutraceutical characteristics.

From the literature review, when the micro-greens were handled with the red and blue Followed, the maximum photosynthesis behavior was observed but the same blue- to red-light ratio was not apparent. Therefore, it is important to recognize specific red and blue combinations of the output of microgreens at under different light intensities.

Carbon Dioxide, Temperature and Humidity

Environmental influences such as carbon dioxide, temperature and humidity play an significant role in plant growth and production during its life cycles. Their rates are common and essential for different plant growth stages. In an experiment to determine the effect of free-air carbon enrichment enhancement and development of cotton (Gossypiumhirsutum), it was observed that enriching carbon dioxide resulted in significant increases in leaves, stems and root photosynthesis and biomass, decreased evapotranspiration, improvements in plant morphology and improved soil respiration.

When studies were performed to evaluate the influence of atmospheric pressure on sugar beet, wheat and kale, the findings showed development of the plants with enhanced atmospheric dampness. The leaf area of sugar beet and kale plants has also been expanded by rising moisture due to the amount of cells. Each plant species would need an ideal temperature to demonstrate the optimum growth and production efficiency of the plant. Two phases of the plant growth are determined by ambient temperature and the soil temperature such as vegetative and reproductive process. For starters, the plant's vegetative growth needs an optimum temperature relative to the reproductive stage.

There are a number of literature regarding the effects on plant growth and production both within (green house), and outside (field) conditions of climatic factors such as carbon dioxide, temperature, and humidity, but no such studies are performed on microgreens. From previous plays, the influence of climatic factors and their management must be taken into account in order to achieve the best growth and production of microgreens grown indoors.

Nutrients

Plants require their growth and production both macro- and micro-nutrients. The vertical agriculture technique involves soil cultivation of plants utilizing a nutrient solution, including inorganic fertilizers for the plant-based soil medium. The Hoagland solution developed by Hoagland and Arnon (1938) is a hydroponic solution that provides all necessary nutrients for plant production.

Commercial crops produced under cultivation produce good quality goods supported by the nutrient solution of a specific crop composition, the growth level, the temperature conditions, the substratum, the or hydroponic method used. The basic method does not however necessarily extend to all crops. When experimenting with continuous nutrient resolution flows in the plants, it was noticed that there is a certain low level below which absorption is no longer feasible at the necessary pace. Luxury intake can contribute to internal toxicity on the other end of concentration. Therefore, nutrients must not be added until the crop needs them to expand. Seeds provide a certain amount of germination nutrients and initial development. While seeds do not immediately need the use of nutrients for germination, they need nutrients to grow and mature correctly. It is therefore important to develop plants with a specific nutrient solution dosage, to decide the ideal dosage, which can be sustained by a growth curve.

In a Brassica microgreens research report, the effect of sole-source LED strength and consistency on the growth and morphology of LED and its contents was used in the 5-day microgreen seeding of 25% Hoagland's No. 1 nutrient solution for critical nutrients such as nitrogen, phosphorus, potassium, calcium, magnesium, iron, manganese, zinc, copper, boron and m. Many specific liquid fertilizers are available commercially on the microgreen market. The 0.4% solution of General Hydroponics Advanced Nutrient Method 2-1-6 ('FloraGro'; 'GhInc., Sebastopol, CA, USA) was used for the 7th day of microgreen growth in an experiment to assess the Nutrient Contenu for chicken and lettuce microgreens grown on vermicompost and hydroponic seed pads. Nevertheless, not many studies have been carried out on microgreen application of industrial liquid fertilizers. The usage of industrial liquid fertilizers comprising all these important nutrients for accelerated microgreen development is also recommended for microgreens.

Container Selection

The container plays an significant role in plant growth by protecting the plants and controlling environmental factors such as temperature, gas exchange and humidity. Microbial degradation may be at risk because high humidity occurs in the sealed tanks that can be sterilized under ultraviolet light for a span of 15 minutes. There could also be a question with gaseous containers closing to be solved with tiny gaps in the diaphragm.

HOW PLANT GROW

All farmers should be able to obtain genetically pure safe seeds, with strong seed vigor and a reasonable percentage of germination. The timely availability of high quality seeds at a fair price guarantees the farmers good yield and benefit. In agriculture, seeds perform a crucial function and are the carriers of the genetic ability of varieties. Creation of quality seed pursuing effective certification procedures plays an significant role in growing our country's food supply. In order to do this, the Government has approved requirements and adopted seed growth, monitoring, certification and marketing methods through the Seeds Act of 1966. In the current situation, demand for approved seeds of high quality significantly exceeds supply availability. This document contains details on the development and purchase of seeds of good quality.

Definition of Seed

Seed is a basic farming product and an egg trapped in the crop tissue. Semiform is often known as a matured ovule consisting of an embryonic plant with a foodstuff and a defensive seed coat surrounding it.

Needs For Plant

The vital needs of a plant are very much like our own - **light, water, air, nutrients**, and a **proper temperature**. The relative value of growing of these needs differs considerably between plants. The capacity of a plant to disperse through a geographical region stems directly from its tolerance to the abiotic and biotic components of the environment. While most habitat components collectively function on a plant and should be used together, the lack of one critical component will decide the plant's wellbeing. If this element is regarded as a restricting element.

The definition of restricting factors encompasses all facets of the relationships between a plant and its environment. Some environmental factor may be a restricting factor. For example, for many species the water is important; most species cannot survive in desert regions due to lack of water and most cannot survive in ponds due to excess water. Extreme temperatures inhibit the growth of plants in many regions; lack of warmth in winter is a limiting factor which restricts many species to tropical areas.

Also, rivalry from animals utilizing the same services is also a restricting factor. The key activity between plants is rivalry. Plants of the same genus are highly competitive because they have the same sunshine, water and nutrients needs.

Many factors in nature help to regulate the development of plants: sunshine, correct temperature, humidity, oxygen and nutrients. Those are classified as environmental influences. The sustainability and efficiency of plant life in each part of a natural or artificial environment. Knowing the underlying truth about how plants function and evolve should allow you to appreciate the plants.

Light: All living organisms, excluding a few bacterial species, rely on their photosynthesis. The mechanism by which green plants grow their own food is photosynthesis. When light energy is available, plants generate food (mostly sugar) in the presence of chlorophyll to release oxygen and water, mixing carbon dioxide with water.

Proper Temperature: The most critical environmental factor that impacts plant growth is temperature. Plants differ in temperature conditions. The plant's capacity to withstand cold temperatures is regarded as robustness. Plants that do not survive cold weather are referred to as tender plants.

Water: Water is important to life. It is one of the most essential plant growth criteria. Water is the principal component of the plant cells; it retains the turgid (rigid) soil, is used for photosynthesis, and it brings nutrients in the field.

Air: Raw materials are used in the development of carbohydrates and proteins that a plant requires to survive and grow. These ingredients are either present in the setting naturally or supplied by the grower. Plants capture and use in photosynthesis the raw material carbon dioxide from the ambient soil.

Nutrients: While plants may use a variety of air nutrients, most of the nutrients a plant requires to remain in the cultivated medium (soil). Throughout the roots of the herb, minerals including nitrogen, potassium, phosphorous, calcium and magnesium are taken.

Environmental Factors Affecting Plant Growth

Light Energy is either absorbed, mirrored or transferred to the surface of a plant. Power is one of the guiding factors in the chemical process known as photosynthesis in the form of sunlight.

Photosynthesis is The mechanism by which green plants create, in the presence of a chlorophyll (white pigment), the food, primarily sugar, from carbon dioxide and water, by utilizing light energy and releasing oxygen and water. The nature, quantity and length of light together affect the development of plants. Plants growing under intense sunshine are usually small and larger and lengthier than in the forest. Semines may begin to develop (germinate) without light, but if they are to continue to expand, the plant emerging from them must have light.

Moisture Water is necessary for development, one of the most critical plant growth requirements. Water is the key component in plant cells, retains the turgid (stiff) plant, it is used for photosynthesis and transfers nutrients through the entire field. Plants often use the water to reduce the leaf temperature, improve the absorption of nutrients and draw water from the roots back into the plants through a mechanism called perspiration.

The hydrologic cycle. The hydrological process is the natural water process. Heat passes through a variety of systems. Water passes by runoff, evaporation, sweat and condensation. The sun offers the strength to shift water in a loop. Everything water on earth, whether it's in a pool, our skin, milk, or underwater, is part of a water process.

Precipitation Either the earth infiltrates (rain, snow, vegetation, etc.) or flows through adjacent ditches or rivers. Water on the lake or pool surface may gradually evaporate from the heat of the sun to form a mist of water. Instead this mist forms a fog which condenses into precipitation. Plants emit water vapor by transpiration into the atmosphere.

Air Carbon dioxide is one of the raw materials used in photosynthesis. The carbon dioxide level of the atmosphere is fairly constant at about 0.03 percent, extremely low, but in the environment around the planet it contributes to about 2 000 000 000 tonnes. The metabolism of plants and livestock, rotting biological products and burning of coal and seismic activity continuously contributes carbon dioxide to the environment. Carbon dioxide diffuses from the environment through the intercellular spaces of the herb through the stomata (pores or openings of the epidermis of plants).

Wind Air is air in transit that can be helpful as well as detrimental to plants. Wind may benefit plants by speeding up heat transmission from leaf surfaces and growing circulation in areas expected to develop fungally. Winds can damage plants by extreme drying, dispersion of weed seeds and often loss of plants.

Proper temperature The atmosphere temperature is the product of heat flow from the surface of the planet to the ambient air. Latitude, altitude and topography differ in temperature. The atmosphere and temperature of an region dictates what plant types are to grow. The capacity of a plant to survive cold temperatures is classified as cold resistant, while plants that cannot withstand cool weather are classified as tender. Temperature varies constantly in the natural world.

Nutrients Plants need 17 specific nutrients, in addition to carbon dioxide and water, to sustain production. Since the most nutrients a plant requires in the soil or rising medium are derived from sunlight, fuel, oxygen and hydrogen. We are separated into macro and micro components. Nitrogen (N) for safe leaves, phosphorus (P) for flower production and potassium (K) for root growth are the key nutrients required in the largest quantities.

The soils on which plants thrive compose of varying amounts of a combination of natural products, organic matter, water and air. The mineral particles fall from rock through lengthy weathering cycles. The biological matter contains living beings, their excretion and decay materials. The hardness of soils relates to the sizes of the prevailing particles. The composition of a surface determines the quantity of dust, water and nutrients in the surface. In fact, dirt, water and roots penetrate much better into soils with large particles (sand). On the other side, water and fertility are primarily caused by the limited size of particles (silt and clay) and organic matter.

Varieties

Several microgreen varieties may be cultivated, but it is most essential that the particular plant is suitable and healthy for human consumption by the farmers. About a hundred different plant species are widely grown in this essential factor and marketed as microgreens (e.g.mustard). The hundreds of historically model varieties of such plants (e.g. Golden Frills mustard, Ruby Streaks mustard or Green Wave Mustard) may not have this number. Microgreens have a fast harvest period although there are varying growth levels across varieties and organisms. Vegetables cultivated as microgreens are ready for harvest in 7-14 days, but herbs cultivated as micrograsses appear to be fairly slow to mature, maturing in 16-25 days.

COMMON SPECIES OF MICROGREENS:

- **Fast growing vegetables** (7 to 14 days)

- cabbage

- corn

- cress

- kale

- kohlrabi

- mustard

- radish

- **Slow growing vegetables** (15 to 25 days)

- amaranth

- arugula

- beet

- carrot

- Swiss chard

- scallion

- **Slow growing herbs** (15 to 30 days)

  - anise

  - basil

  - cilantro

  - dill

  - fennel

  - parsley

  - saltwort

  - shisho

  - sorrel

NOTES:

Regardless of every plants you cultivate, appropriate sanitary facilities and protocols should be practiced to avoid cross-contamination between organisms for the health of consumers with allergies.

Methods of production

Growers need to determine how they want their crops to be developed. Each method of development has its advantages, upkeep and difficulties. The following processing methods have been used to grow microgreens on a commercial scale:

• **Soil-based**

  * garden beds

  * raised planters

• **Various forms of hydroponic crop production**

Community of substrates in which the roots inside pH expand with neutral media.

Community of solutions in which the roots expand in nutrient solutions.

Technique for nutrient film (NFT) where the roots are planted in a continuous current of nutrient richwater (nutrient solution).

Aeroponics in which mineral solution is stored and misted in the root network.

The development processes are usually the same regard of the factory. However, the processing of microgreens needs a food-safe environment, compliant with local requirements and regulations.

STAGES OF PRODUCTION

Seed sources

Is the output of microgreens strong in seed compared with traditional crop growth? The cost-effective seed will bring a great deal to the manufacturing costs and in certain situations it would be the turning point between the appropriate commodity or not. It has more than one drawback, food protection and traceability issues. It is advised that a distributor of vendors give their goods traceability, food health guarantee and/or environmental certifications.

Seed storage and preparation

Seeds should be stored in safe containers in an sealed environment to prevent pollution or insect problems. Seeds should be stored in cool (1 to 5 ° C), dry (3 to 10 percent relative humidity), dark locations to ensure optimum efficiency. Seeds should not be permitted to rehydrate during storage; otherwise the germination cycle may begin prematurely and eventually decrease seeder viability. Some seed species may need to be immersed in water (immersed seeds) or in antacid (scarification used to split the hard seed surface of other plants) in order for germination to occur.

Growing species has specific for germination requirements, and it is important that producers know their species and their spread requirements. Soaking solutions including distilled hydrogen peroxide can also be used as disinfectants, reducing the chance that the seeds may bring of pathogen and bacterial infection. Similarly, the handling of hot water may also lead to the disinfection of certain seeds such as arugula, basil, chia, cress and flax. Contact with water can allow this sort of seed to develop a dense coating with a gluey / gel material on the surface of the seed. This coating tends to retain humidity and allow the germination of the seed simpler. Growing these seeds may entail additional measures and cautious germination. Until planting, mucilaginous seeds need not be need sacked.

Seeding

Regardless of the planting medium, seeds shall be manually shook or scattered uniformly, at the density of the form of seed and the required finished product. To retain moisture after planting, farmers shall apply a thin layer of fine vermiculite, a single-ply sheet, or a thin layer of soil-less planting surface on top of the seeds. Regarding rising seeding densities see the list below.

Common seeding densities

- **100 g to 120 g**

  - sunflower

  - peas

  - corn

- **60 g to 70 g**

  - mustard

  - broccoli

  - radish

  - Swiss chard

  - red cabbage

- **50 g to 60 g**

  - dill

  - basil

  - arugula

Germination and growth

A grower must become a master to replicate the ecosystem and the conditions that seed requires to germinate in order to produce microgreens. This solution may include the use of heating matts, extra lighting or complete darkness, less or more watering depending on the plant.

Environment: The optimum microgreen-production climate may be variety-specific, but the most requested plantes should reach a desirable temperature range of 18 to 24 ° C and a relative humidity(RH) of 40 to 60 percent. Rising temperature and humidity may increase the likelihood of pest and disease outbreaks. Good air ventilation (mixing, diffusion and drainage) is a must in any increasing setting. Air ventilation helps create a constant temperature and humidity in the growing region. Growers need to combine and match throughout a growing region horizontal air fans with compressed air or natural air winds. In case plants are grown in a vertical racking device, caution must be taken to insure that air movement between layers is easily retained or otherwise trapped between layers. Airflow for such systems may be operated with several smaller ventilators connected to the rack systems at any growth point.

Lighting: Most plants react differently to artificial light than to natural light. Learn the period of light, temperature and size of the field. Of example, if the source of light is too far from the flower, it can occur stretching or "legality." Crop colourm can also look washed out where light strength is not adequate. Some lighting devices produce heat during service, such as some fluorescent lamps. When an building contains 150 + fluorescent lamps, it will affect the ambient temperature significantly. In recent years, the usage of LEDs in sealed manufacturing plants, such as factories, has been more prevalent owing to reduced heat exposure and the prospect of changing the light spectrum for some cultivations. Lights that work in a greenhouse setting for 12 to 18 hours a day to substitute natural sunlight, and four to six hours a day for supplementary illumination.

The energy required for LED lighting systems was significantly less than for fluorescent and halogenic alternatives. The initial cost of LED lighting systems, despite significant cost reductions in the last few years, may still be prohibiting large. In order to guarantee a successful enterprise, farmers and future growers should have a clear idea of the estimated capital and operational costs of growing micro-greens before development.

Watering: The development of microgreen includes continuous and measured irrigation of plants. For the initial germination of the seed, misting nozzles are advised to prevent the seed displacements. Shower head nozzles can be added at a point of irrigation in order to satisfy elevated water demands of the plants. Irrespective of the facility, adequate floor drainage will be in position to tackle excess water from the water from the field. Flooring water may be a breeding ground for insects and pathogens and a possible health threat for operating.

Harvesting

Micro-green processing is a big phase in the manufacturing cycle and may require a lot of time and effort. Due to the small scale of such "tiny" seeds, processing is very challenging and requires to be treated with caution. Cooling is needed and suggested for preserving freshness after harvest, consistency of production and good food protection practices as soon as possible. Micro-greens usually are harvested as near to the stem base without contaminating the finished product by growing medium or seeds. Bear in mind that the simpler the harvesting devices are, the quicker they are to be properly sanitized.

The method of cutting microgreens depends on the production size, but the following methods are common:

• pair of scissors

• electric knife

• very sharp chef's knife

• hand-held harvesting mechanism

• automated harvesting conveyor system

The crop may be cut directly through the final package, but micrograins which are collected are often washed before package more often than ever. When you wash the microgreens, make sure you grow them in correctly sanitized storage bins.

If you sell or harvest your microgreens for plants, you will be required to get a food handling permit and operate in an licensed food facility. Be sure to review before development the local and regional laws and specifications.

The finished microgreen product shape differs, but most commonly:

• fresh cut produce/harvested microgreens

• living tray microgreens/live plant sales

• mixed microgreen combinations

• value-added/processed products that include

Microgreens

Washing and drying

Washing microgreens is both a very careful move and a value added benefit for your company. The method reassures consumers that their food has been washed and ready for use. However, microgreens are mostly processed without any preparation or frying, so it is therefore presumed that the microgreen items left behind can be ingested in the same manner as it is. Micro greens must be correctly and completely dried to reduce the possibility of microbial growth and pollution and no excessive gaps during processing, washing, drying and packing should be permitted to improve shelf life.

NATURAL PEST AND DISEASE CONTROL

What is natural pest and disease control?

The natural ecosystem structure involves rodents and pathogens. There is a balance between predators and pests in this framework. That is the way humans are governed by nature. The animals we consider pests and the disease-causing species are plagues and viruses as their actions destroy crops and impact yields. Because they become unbalanced, one person will become optimistic because they are not vulnerable to them. The aim of natural control is to preserve the equilibrium between pest and predator and to sustain an appropriate level of pests and diseases. They are not completely abolished, as they do have a place in the natural world. The destruction can not be remedied and management is more impossible until a pest or disease starts to strike a crop. Using methods, when appropriate, to minimize or deter attacks on pest and disease.

INTEGRATED PEST MANAGEMENT

IPM in protected cultivation

The emergence, production and management of pests and diseases under greenhouse systems is definitely affected by the inclusion of crops. The dynamic control systems for modern greenhouses are engineered to sustain a cost-effective and physiological condition for the crop. The requirements therefore insure that pests and diseases have a safe, healthy environment: high humidity and temperature, no rain or wind. Therefore, rodents and diseases may be more aggressive and do more harm in greenhouses than in open field settings. Moreover, opposed to open field agriculture, when inadvertently or intentionally added, natural enemies may be rare or entirely missing, whereas the protection of the greenhouse climate enables natural enemies of pests to be used as an efficient control tool.

Pest and disease management will develop appropriately as crop production practices become advanced. A variety of innovative new technologies have been implemented in recent years for rising plants (e.g. soilless technologies). If a production technique evolves, insect and disease species may be introduced to a different environment. Improvements to conventional management practices may be needed in response. Greenhouses need exemplary plant security strategies for certain purposes. Due to economical considerations linked to the high degree of skill needed for business performance, rotation cannot usually be performed in greenhouses. The same crop or crops are therefore cultivated year after year; careful caution should therefore be exercised especially with regard to the insect, which remains in the soil or the framework of the greenhouse itself.

Because the importance of greenhouse plants is typically high, expensive steps to regulate pesticides can be economically justified in order to reach the necessary minimum standards. In general, greater caution is required for the use and application of pesticides in greenhouse plants in order to prevent photonic effects or pesticide residue. Chemical regulation in prophylactic treatments can be quickly added if a clean crop is required (for example, ornamentals). Ornamentals have a strong esthetic value and a compromised flora is unstable; even though they are shipped to countries with zero tolerance laws, or only at a small infestation point, they lose their appeal. However, any infestation can typically be accepted for most other plants, as it contributes too little to no harm.

In contrast to other industries, many of the latest, non-chemical management methods are now in use in greenhouses within the context of the IPM programmers. An incorporation of environmental, economic, biological, mechanical and physical restrictions on pests and diseases with a wide-ranging approach to preserving greenhouse crops would be confusing, rendering beneficial improvements to pests and pathogens less possible. IPM is currently being used in more than 95% of the greenhouse crops and ornamental production region in northern Europe.

PREVENTIVE MEASURES

Based on crop form and region of output, a broad variety of reduction methods may be implemented. Cultural control was essential in the defense of greenhouse crops before the advent of chemical control. Today farmers are accused of not being common with safe crops with effective methods of cultural control such as crop rotation. In comparison, strategies such as mixed cropping, simultaneous cropping and trap harvesting in greenhouses are seldom utilized. Pest management and mechanical / physical monitoring may be called part of cultural regulations and are frequently used in greenhouses. At first, mechanical control was focused on weed elimination and infested plant sections (e.g. destruction of leaf miner larvae mines). However, it has been interested in recent years in the usage of fine mesh insect networks on all greenhouse aeration openings, as well as the development of protection access systems (SAS) to eliminate dangerous diseases and vectors. Physical regulation to clean the soil is added. One method of cultural control is the management of the crop's ecosystem to deter or mitigate disease by computer models designed to forecast the optimum greenhouse climate for crop growth and to recognize disease controls. Host disease-resistant plants are used extensively. While eradication of a recently introduced disease and its costs are very large, eradication in the greenhouse is often simpler than in the open field.

Inspection and quarantine

Pests grow to their greatest degree in the origin centers of different crop plants. Therefore, certain pests are concentrated in particular areas and the management of them is in the general interest of agriculture. Crop plants often invade new areas without several of their pests and pathogen, and these crops perform well in the new areas. Most of this benefit is gradually lost, though, as pests and diseases appear sooner or later to invade the seed.

To eliminate or reduce the occurrence of invasive tropical insect pests, there are detailed laws and recommendations on the safety conditions of the plants transported. The prevention of pests and diseases by regulations is highly necessary and plant safety programs in many countries include health certificates.

Measures at greenhouse level

Rotavators are used in greenhouses for the preparation of soils: they create very fine soil spores, contributing to high weed seed germination. Black and white plastic mulching is an effective means of managing weeds and certain insect pests (thrips, leaf mines, etc.) whether used on locally or through the entire greenhouse (total mulching). Certain safety steps during the growth season require manual collection before weeds set seed.

At the conclusion of the previous crop process, protective measures (for the current harvest) may be taken using solarization to reduce the soil pests and disease inoculums. After many years of full avoidance the infestation is very small, the soil decreases to acceptable levels of plague and pathogen inoculums.

HOST PLANT RESISTANCE

Plants may respond to different abiotic and biotic conditions within their natural setting. For example, high altitudes (abiotic stresses) or herbivores or pathogens (biotic stresses). Resistance may be dependent on various mechanisms: antixenosis (characteristics that decrease herbivorcolonisation) or antibiosis (characteristics that destroy or eliminate herbivores after landing and eating) Cries have been studied for centuries for improved consistency and stronger yields. In the past, seed was purposely collected from plants with lower diagnostic symptoms. Currently industrial breeding ambitions have contributed to vulnerable varieties of increased growth and cultural efficiency, integrating the usage of pesticides in the selection fields. Hospitality for insecticides also needs to grow more, although for other cultivars the usage of disease-resistant cultivars is also highly advanced. The use of disease-resistant cultivars is in principle the simplest and most reliable way to combat disease and would preferably be immune to all crop diseases. Nevertheless, in fact, there are very few crops in which only a small proportion of the cultivars withstand more than a limited number of diseases.

Unfortunately, a variety of pathogens occur as varieties, each with specific virulence genes such that a cultivar may be immune or susceptible to some but not all varieties of the pathogen. Immune crops typically stay disease-free very briefly, new pathogen strains grow, or the pathogen population becomes a mixture of several separate strains predominating with one or more. The equilibrium of the pathogen strains also responds rapidly to shifts in the host community. Whether a pathogen population is a mixture of different strains with certain in extremely small proportion is difficult, if not impossible to ascertain, or whether a pathogen develops virulent mutations at in regular intervals that are generally lost from the community without an adequate resistant host on which to cultivate. Often, while these mutants are able to develop in resistant cultivars, they cannot cope and thrive with other trains, since they are less healthy. But some new resistant cultivars lose their tolerance easily for multiple causes. A more rational solution, albeit easier and more time intensive, is to mix as many genes as possible. That form of tolerance would be disrupted if the pathogen creates a dynamic battle that overcomes the resistant genes concurrently. A variety of viruses are immune varieties. Total and enduring resistance in breeding programs, though, is challenging to obtain.

However, pests and diseases that adapt to the resistance of the plant host, a process that is similar to the adaptation of pests to pesticides. Adaptation happens in particular where the resistance is increasing, the heritage is simple and the cultivar is reactive. Awareness of the nature of the pest or pathogen species involved is therefore important. Fortunately, the tolerance to insects is mostly incomplete and its heritage is polygenic, which allows it less difficult to choose tolerance-adapted biotypes. Nevertheless, recent advances in breeding with tolerance such as the cultivation of transgenic plants bearing BacilusThuringiensis toxic genes continue to rely on very high-expression monogenic factors.

BIOLOGICAL CONTROL OF INSECTS AND MITE PESTS

This segment discusses a few general concerns relating to biocontrol: what is biocontrol, why is it essential, which organic forms are seen as controversy and which biocontrol methods are available? Presented are the proposals for a biological surveillance scheme and a method for testing natural enemies until their implementation.

Biological restrictions on plant pests are laid down because they differ from insects and mites, certain pest species (nematodes, viruses and weeds) are often handled quickly, as growth in these areas is late, at least for greenhouse crops.

Definition

Virtually all insect management steps except industrial pesticides are protected by the word "biological protection." This is now widely recognized that the word "use of living organisms as pest control agents" should be specified, which suggests a human involvement.

• Environmental control: possible predators in nature are maintained by their existing enemies at low densities.

• Biological control: natural targets (e.g. mice, killer bugs or parasitic wasps) are fairly large species.

Microbial control: micro-organisms (e.g. microbes, fungi, protozoa, nematodes', or viruses) are potential rivals.

• Biotechnical regulation: Pheromonal attraction, sterile strategies of sterile genetic management, chemical regulation of youthful hormones and host plant resistance are all biotechnological strategies.

Genetic regulation and monitoring of attractants, repellents, anti-food goods and pheromones (a specific desirable category) are not typical ingredients.

History of biological control in greenhouse crops

Efficient greenhouse development needs well-trained farmers who are not willing to take risk of insect harm on political grounds: they would definitely do it when chemical tests are handled better and cheaper. Despite this, biological pesticide management in greenhouses has been in operation for nearly 45 years with commercial success. Growers readily agreed and now depend on its implementation. A main explanation for the accelerated growth of biological protection strategies was the presence of pesticide tolerance in a few primary greenhouse pests. More than 30 varieties of natural enemies against more than 22 varieties of pests have been implemented over the last 45 years. The greenhouse field for biological monitoring has now expanded from 400 ha in 1970 to more than 50 000 ha. Today, biological regulation of the major greenhouse pests is introduced in more than 25 countries in a total of 35 greenhouse-industries nations.

Biological and Microbial Control Agents

The use of unique natural insect enemies, specifically chosen and tested, to eradicate species which may pose a danger to other valuable organisms, is vital to modern biological management.

Predators

Human animals consume a variety of prey and look for food throughout their lives. Some animals are polyphagous and eat a wide variety of beasts, others are oligaphagous (narrower) or monophagous (extremist). The polyphagous arthropod predators do not rely on the intended species and prefer to feed on the animals that are more plentiful and quickly caught. Monophagous and oligaphagous parasitic predators are more likely to be suitable for biological surveillance. For greenhouse biological management systems several specific types of pests are included.

Parasitoids

Those insects (many of them monophagous) parasitically grow into a single host that is inevitably destroyed. They comprise a surprisingly large community of small wasps and flies with approximately 300 000 species identified. The adults are extremely mobile and live-free and will actively hunt for hosts to lay eggs. The larvae live in (endoparasitoid) or host (ectoparasitoid), until they develop up entirely (egg, larvae and pupal stage), typically destroying their host as they are being depopulated. A variety of parasitoid plants are used in greenhouses for pest control.

Pathogens

Parasite microorganisms are always likely to destroy their host. Dead hosts emit millions of individual microbes spread via the wind and vectors. Protozoans have a typically longer-term effect on pests. Pathogens are readily mass processed and release systems are close to the usage of industrial pesticides.

Bacteria

Almost all bacteria currently in use of microbial insecticides are Bacillus organisms. Some bacteria are pathogenic to animals, but often possibly dangerous to humans or hard to large. In certain instances, once food is consumed, bacteria impact their hosts and also develop toxic metabolites that destroy the intestinal wall. The most common and popular species is B.

Thuringiensis (Bt). Thuringiensis. The time before the intake of a lethal dosage ranges from hours and a day or two. However, the bug ceases feed within hours and at sub lethal doses. Its toxin is commonly used in greenhouse biocontrol for caterpillar regulation and was involved in the production of several transgenic plants (primarily field crops).

Viruses

Viruses do not exist easily and may only reproduce in living host cells. There are at least seven virus families including insect pathogens. The Baculoviridae family is peculiar because it is specific to invertebrates and has little similarity to invertebrates, systemic or biochemical. Baculoviruses are especially appropriate for biological regulation in terms of protection and because of their pesticide ability. Baculoviridae may be used to manage diseases caused by Lepidoptera larvae. The larvae die 4–8 days after infection and the putrefying cadaver releases millions of virus pieces. In greenhouses, an NPV is used to monitor larvae of Spodopteraexigua (Nuclear Polyhedrosis Virus). Since all of these viruses are easily deactivated by UV radiation of 180 to 320 nm, the light-spectrum component absorbs the glass and plastic sheet and the usage of viruses in greenhouses may be quite effective.

Fungi

Fungi are the only insect diseases to enter the cuticle – the most growing source of infection. Such species, such as aphids and scales, eat by biting, are thus often targeted by fungal pathogens. Fungi are therefore highly dependent on environmental conditions, especially high humidity, for infection. Most fungal achievements have been with deuteromycetes, which induce only in tropical ecosystems epizootic vegetation feeding insects. Two fungal agents against whiteflies are used in greenhouses: Verticilliumlecanii and Aschersoniaaleyrodis; the more general fungus;V. Lecanii is also used for aphid and thrip control.

Nematodes

Steinernematidae tribe – Heterorhabditis and Steinernema(Neoplectana) are the most popular nematodes. They are distinguished by an interaction with Xenorhabdusgenus bacteria. Infective minors bear shared bacteria in their intestines and activate the bacterial cells that spread and destroy insects within 48 hours of reaching the hostrum (through natural openings). These nematodes are virulent, destroy hosts quickly and are easily developed in vivo and in vitro;

they have a very wide variety of host systems. Both classes are used in biocontrol systems for greenhouses.

METHODS OF RELEASE OF BIOLOGICAL AGENTS

Parasitoids, predators and pathogens, as mentioned below, may be used in different kinds of biological control programs.

Inoculative biological control

Beneficial species are captured and published (only in small numbers) in a research environment where there is an insect. The techniques are used to eradicate pesticides long-term and usually natural rivals (which are then found in the pest's region of origin). The first universal method of biological control, also called "classical" biological control, does not occur for greenhouse plants because permanent biocontrol can be stopped from cultivating unregulated crops: the crop is eliminated, its pesticides and natural enemies at the end of each growing season.

Inundative biological control

Indigenous or imported beneficial species are mass-reared in labs or acquired by specialist biological control firms and routinely discharged in vast amounts to achieve rapid disease management for one or two centuries, e.g. usage as a biotic insecticide. The widespread usage of large amounts of parasitic mites

(Amblyseiusspp.) against thrips (Frankliniellasp.) in safe cultivation is one illustration of this method.

Seasonal inoculative biological control

Indigenous or imported natural enemies are mass reared or purchased from the foreign market and are regularly released against pests in shorter crops (3-10 months), so protection results will continue for many years. A significant number of natural enemies are released, plus the natural enemy's population to be managed later this season to maintain immediate power. This approach varies significantly from flood management as it seeks to provide an influence across many generations and thus involves inoculative regulation. The biological exploitation of Tutaabsolutato Europe (2006), North Africa (2008) and the Near East (2009–10) with the native (originally Latin America) parasite of Trichogrammaacheae is demonstrated by this method.

Conservation

Conservation is an alternative tool for intervention on natural enemy's conservation; it may contribute to a wider variety of desirable organisms as well as to greater numbers of each plant, contributing to increased pest management. In the natural environments around greenhouses, for example, leaf miners and aphids may move into protective structures to have sufficient power. Therefore, careful management of the crops and the greenhouse conditions will enhance or restore natural regulation.

How to implement a biological controlprogramme

Planning the biological control programme

A system summary is made, describing both the target organism's taxonomic and noxious status (pest species or weed). Knowledge is gathered on the ecology of the insect and its natural enemies by literature study and correspondence. When the foreign market will not have a suitable natural enemy available, discovery must take place and an array of natural enemies must continue with the exposure to the genetic variation features of the natural enemy and to the selection of appropriate specimens.

The value of a natural enemy to the exploration region is defined by the analysis of host selection and harmful traits (e.g. hyperparasite behaviors, poliphagy). Based on such details, an initial collection of organisms for potential studies may be made. While research in the field of discovery cannot usually be focused on predicting the establishment or efficacy of new natural enemy organisms in a new setting, they help to decide if an agent is clearly unsuitable for specific areas. Following the initial collection, a thorough analysis of the suitable species is undertaken. The chosen stock is packed for shipping and then the natural enemy in the world where the disease is to be regulated is mass manufactured and published. A final performance evaluation will then be carried out within the goal region.

Shipment of natural enemies

Throughout different stages of growth, entomophagous insects and acari may be brought into the greenhouse:

• Eggs (e.g. *Chrysoperla*)

• Larvae or nymphs (e.g. *Orius, Phytoseiulus*)

• pupae (e.g. *Trichogramma, Encarsia, Eretmocerus*)

• adults (e.g. *Aphidius, Diglyphus*)

• all stages (e.g. *Amblyseius*)

The stage they are released depends mainly on transport and handling in the greenhouse;

transportation and release sometimes happens while they are least subjected to mechanical handling, i.e. Egg or pupal period. Pupal stage. If it is challenging, but necessary, to discern the natural enemy from the parasite (host), then adults are the only remedy. Release of adult parasitoids is not advised and release is exceedingly challenging, sometimes contributing to decreased fertility relative to released juvenile parasitoids.

Release of natural enemies

A variety of approaches are required to incorporate the greenhouse. Eggs and pupae may be spread over the greenhouse on a typical plant (such as the host plant's leaves, for example Chrysoperla and Encarsia) or on paper or carton boards (such as Encarsia, Trichogramma and Eretmocerus). Human enemies may also be gathered in these stages and stored in containers which are then transported to the greenhouse (e.g. nesidiocorris).

Natural enemies in a traveling process (larvae, nymphs, or adults) should be placed in a greenhouse in containers in which the grower may disperse or spray them on plants (e.g., several adult parasitos and predators). For advice concerning the appropriate handling (especially after pick-up from airport on arrival of shipment); timely distribution (time from airport to land distribution); and release(practical handling of containers) of beneficial insects, biological control agencies, distributors and extension services should be consulted. Nonetheless, in very recently adopted countries, adequate guidance on biological controls – a weak point in the biological control chains – is scarcely accessible.

Risks of biological control

Recent understanding shows that the harmful consequences of industrial pesticide use exceed the biological regulation threats. Nonetheless, the dangers of utilizing natural enemies to manage pests are addressed here.

Environmental risks

No natural insect enemies that are used for biological insect pest management are specifically toxic to humans. However, they may pose environmental threats (e.g. assaults on certain beneficial organisms). Many animals are transferred from one part of the planet to another. Although future natural enemies are tested for probable adverse consequences in the area of implementation, it can never be determined with utter confidence that a natural enemy does not alter behavior, targeting some other beneficial species or healthy occupants of the same environment.

Risks of resistance

With respect to resistance, a host lives with many defensive mechanisms to prevent predation or parasitism. As well as behavioral defense (hiding position hunt, firm body motions to deter assaults, vomiting, etc) and morphological defense (e.g. thick cuticle development), many host species possess an internal parasitoid defensive mechanism: the encapsulation of parasitoid larvae. Complete production of host tolerance to the parasitoid organisms is extremely uncommon in biological control although encapsulation is very widespread in many insect classes. Frequent production by pests of insecticide tolerance is a natural enemy occurrence not observed in the past45 years. The co-evolution between natural enemies and hosts is believed to avoid the creation between full tolerances to enemies by pests. Extensive parasitoid strain, host selection is constant for the ability to encapsulate parasitoid eggs. Parasitoids with the potential to avoid encapsulation are often continuously chosen. Of example, this mutual selection mechanism does not occur in a host-pesticide partnership.

PRACTICAL BIOLOGICAL CONTROL OF INSECTS AND MITES

Biologic measures are used against large greenhouse pests and other pathogens, including regular inoculative releases and strategies to improve and preserve natural enemies. In general, companies commercializing biological protection agents have the decision threshold and amount of natural enemies required for the management of various pests.

Whiteflies

T's biological influence.Vaporariorum with regular theparasitoidinoculative releases, Encarsiaformosa is commonly utilized in temperate areas and to an even greater degree in hot regions in greenhouses. Still, E. The not so successful inoculative release of the pest, Macrolophuscaliginosus is a complementary method under cool cloudy conditions. In addition, the inoculation of both natural enemies now used just E in several greenhouses. T initial communities.Formosa Was published. Whitefly movement between crops is occurring, needing higher densities of natural enemies but for shorter rising seasons. Formosa does don't test B. Now, a mixture of predatorymitis, Amblyseiusswirski, predatory worm, Nesidiocorristenuis and parasitoids,

Eretmoceruseremicus and E. Applied to regulate T, mundus.B-vaporariorum.In warm areas, tobacco greenhouse crops.

Leaf miners

Diglyphusisaea are done inoculative releases commercially in greenhouse crops for biological monitoring leaf miners. This is combined with Dacnusasibirica in cold areas. Natural colonies of leaf miners in warm areas are plentiful all year round, and leaf miners are regulated easily by natural parasitism (up to 80 percent). Additional releases of D. Isaea are made only when natural parasitism is small, especially when greenhouse mesh screening is applied.

Aphids

All the aphid species that attack greenhouse crops, including the parasitoid Aphidiuscolemani and predators, such as AphidoletesaphidimiyzaandChrysoperlacarnea, are suitable natural enemies available. In warmer regions, aphids do not normally reach economic thresholds due to the presence of indigenous population of their natural enemies, without use of broad-spectrum insecticides or fine mesh screens.

Mites

Biological control of phytoseiuluspersimilison tomato mites was largely ineffective and is not widely used. Nonetheless, the new species of predatory mite Amblyseiusswirskiand a new strain of P. persimilis (Strain T).

Caterpillars

Chrysodeixischalcites, Autograph Gamma, Spodopteralittoralis are held thuringiensis treatments. Helicoverpaarmigerais, too, well monitored, so that care is administered while there are eggs or youthful larvae. The Trichogramma evanescens are inoculative releases are often rendered for the biological regulation of C. Any greenhouse crops include chalcites.

PHYSICAL CONTROL

Heat management or radiation protection of rodents and pathogens is referred to as physical regulation. Heat treatment is used for suppression of unhealthy bacteria in surface water; farmers also use special equipment to combat the weed stroke. Certain techniques are required to clean water. Manufacturing processes of root and stem pathogens occurrence will be specifically sanitized. Throughout the non-cropping season in summer, all manufacturing industries benefit from passive solarization: systems are fully sealed despite weathering surfaces; temperatures of $> 50\ ^\circ$ C are important for the eradication or at least the reduction of pathogens or other pests in production facilities.

Chemical soil disinfection may be done in order to establish soil plants free of pests and pathogens. However, cultural and physical approaches, such as steam sterilization and solarisation, should be utilized first if possible.

Sterilization of soil

Soil therapy is regarded as soil sterilization, although this is not exclusively true, because only the most successful cure will not remove all living species, and the soil is not completely sterile. The most general words are partial sterilization or pasteurization and accomplished by steam sterilization or solarisation.

Solarization

Solarization is conveniently coupled with other monitoring strategies to common chemical regulation requirements. In conjunction with decreased dose of chemical fumigants, it increases the management of soil transmitted diseases, which are otherwise difficult to monitor. Solarization, which involves the usage of biocontrol agents, has strong potential and allows antagonists simpler to implement, in particular in warm areas. Solarization is a type of soil pasteurization by concentrating plastic sheets of solar energy into the earth surface. This is a simple and effective method of pasteurizing crops, weeds and other pests and managing them. This is, however, only efficient when at least 30 days of strong solar radiation are possible and thus should not be utilized in colder environments during the hot season if there is no covered crop situation. The soil has to be humidified (water retaining capacity) to insure that the stored energy stays beneath the surface of the soil. A layer of polyethylene avoids transpiration and the release into the sun. Transparent plastic raises the soil's temperature through the greenhouse impact it induces. Greenhouse impact with black and opaque plastic is missing The thermal penetration depth (and thus effectiveness) is increased by increasing the solarisation cycle. The temperature rise in the top soil is around 10 ° C and the deepness decreases.

To effectively suppress weeds, a 4-6 week solarization cycle (depending on the radiation) is required. The results with perennial weed species are noted as good. Soil solarization is a promising strategy and may have a significant future in many countries (especially with the phase-out of Montreal-protocol's methyl bromide). Initially utilized even in hot regions throughout the summer, due to technical advancements solarisation spreads to colder places and colder seasons. Soil regulates various diseases, including Colletotrich, F. Soil solarization regulates. f. Oxyspor f. Splitter, V. dahliae, P. lycopersici and R. Solani. Solani. The number of meloidogynesp declines as do other plant greenhouse insects that pupate in soil in greenhouse plants (Liriomyzaspp.,Tutaabsoluta, Frankliniel laoccidentalis etc.). Using correctly, the application of fumigants greatly reduces surface solarisation.

Solarizing tomato stakes and hooks is an effective way to monitor some diseases like Didymellastem cancer and can easily be collected during the hot months of the year by processing the agricultural content in vacuum plastic greenhouses. In colder regions, major killing can be accomplished by actually shutting the greenhouse in the after-season (space solarisation) of viruses and insects and mite pests. Solarization of container material, such as peat, provides the possibility for recycling these items. Unfortunately, this natural control strategy is only utilized in full by a small number of countries, especially in warm regions.

Agronomic benefits of soil solarization

In addition to removing such pests, solarisation often improves the yields. In non-infested solar heated soils, change in plant growth has been noted. One cause for improved growth is that minerals are released during soil sterilization (partial or complete), and the soil's nutritional condition improves. The existence of elevated concentrations of NO3, NH4 +, Ca2 +, Mg2 +, K + and soluble organic matter is verified by chemical and physical analyzes of solar-heated soils. The stimulation of beneficial microorganisms is another reason for increased plant growth after solarisation: many saprophytes (particularly heat tolerant ones) thrive better during solarisation than most pathogenic ones.

Steam treatment

For almost a century, greenhouse cultivators have used soil disinfestation using steam. Pathogenic plants are removed by steaming and even weed seeds are annihilated (high costs mean, however, that they cannot just be used for weed control). Soil steaming often promotes crop growth before planting. Soil heat treatment at 100 ° C is the most efficient soil sterilization process. At this altitude, bacterial and fungal infections, nematodes and even soil-borne viruses are silenced. The sustained temperature of 70 ° C is, on the other side, appropriate for fungal infections, bacterial infections and nematodes to monitor. Soil steam treatment methods include: surface steaming, drain steam and negative pressure vapour.

Sheet steaming

Steam is pumped under a sheet covering the soil. The performance rate is dependent on the form, cultivation and humidity of the soil. The soil should be dry and treated as thoroughly as practicable before the steam is applied to encourage penetration. This approach works in clay soils, but the necessary temperature of 70 ° C is reached in sand and loam soil only in the upper soil layers and pathogens live in the deeper layers. The disinfestation of dense soils is normally very complicated because of their capacity to conserve water.

Drain steam system

A new method has now been built to increase the temperature range at greater depths – drain pipes submerged at a depth between 50–60 cm and 80 cm, from which the the steam can be driven. This method is complex, inefficient and not generally accepted.

Negative pressure steaming

Negative pressure steaming is a modern method: steam is deposited in the soil covering layer and pulated into the soil through the fan into perforated polypropene pipes by means of a negative pressure air pumped out from the soil. A major change in new techniques is negative pressure steaming. Compared to sheet steaming, it has equal or superior temperature range; it saves fuel and has smaller investments in drainage. It may therefore be inferred that negative pressure vaporization is the most effective steam method for all soil forms. Damp sterilization of soil is safer than industrial disinfection for productive cultivation.

Disinfection methods for water

The transition from seed to seed did not allow crop-borne diseases to vanish. Some root-infecting diseases are often present in new crops. There is also a chance of transmitting root infecting diseases in a closed network requiring the recirculation of drain water. In order to prevent disease transmission, drain water may flow into the holding tank from the rising source, where it is disinfected before reuse. The soil as well as the rainwater sources that be polluted by plant pests, bacteria and viruses; thus, the entire source of water will first be disinfected.

Heat treatment

The successful management of fungal, bacterial and viral diseases may be accomplished by heat treatment. A temperature of 90 ° C is advised for 30 seconds. Heat exchangers have energy conservation.

Oxidation

Oxidation by ozone or UV radiation is an effective tool for water disinfestation. Ozone is inactivating human pathogenic viruses and microbes, the fastest oxidizing factor. As a donor of electrons (oxidation) to other compounds, ozone itself reduces to oxygen and thus can remove mung, bacteria and viruses. Ultraviolet radiation, particularly UV rays with short wavelengths of wavelength from200 to 280 nm, kills micro-organisms through photochemical reactions.

Water filtration

Water filtration is required for targeted phytophthorasp disinfestations. It has been used for over a century to purify drinking water. In studies for their efficacy against plant-pathogenic fungi, Fusarium oxysporum could not be respected as the membrane could easily be transmitted via the micro conidia. A variation in the flow rate or new materials may increase effectiveness. The multiple ultrafiltration membrane with a polar size of 0,001 μm has been used for complete water disinfestation however for a number of technological reasons including membrane blockage, the procedure is not appropriate for greenhouses.

MECHANICAL CONTROL

Mechanical insect vector control involves the use of insect isolation cages, color sticky bands and water-bearing pheromone traps. Mechanical controls also impact weeds and diseases.

Using insect screens for mechanical exclusion of insect pests and vectors

The invasion of insects through ventilation openings will discourage or reduce the intrusion of pests by the installation of screens on the ventilation openings. Thrips are not used in screens with a mesh size of 0.15 mm; 0.35 mm holds fly and aphid; 0.8 mm is appropriate for leaf miners. Screens do not suppress the pests; they simply exclude most of them; it must therefore be installed in advance of the appearance of pests and additional pest control measures, such as intelligent chemical control and biocontrol, must be taken. The safety of crops from arthropods is considered more important than protecting them from nature, so that physical exclusion of insects from greenhouse will help to reduce direct crop harm and the occurrence of insect transmission insecticide and predator can still immigrate via screens into the greenhouse; unfortunately larger ones cannot. In principle, the exclusion can be accomplished by mounting screens with a mesh gap wider than the insect's side of the body width and the openings and doors of the ventilation on the roof; in practice, some insect intrusion persists.

However, it should be noted that the use of screens could hamper ventilation, leading to overheating and increased humidity that promote plant stress and susceptibility to pests and diseases. Improved moisture needs more fungicide sprays than in an unscreened greenhouse before. Screens often reduce the absorption of energy, and it is necessary to sacrifice the control of energy, temperature and moisture to prevent any detrimental effects on plants and their vulnerability to diseases. Forced ventilation may be used to mitigate such harmful effects, but it can only drag small insects through the glass. While screens may decrease immigrant pesticide levels, they also minimize the influx of valuable arthropods. Complete omission in neither event. Unfortunately, when combined with poisoning in warm regions, the use of fine mesh screens seriously impedes greenhouse ventilation.

Types of screens

Various kinds of screen are designed to defend plants from insects; the task of the grower is to respond to the local circumstances (climate and insect populations).

Woven screens

Conventional cloth screens are constructed of simple cloth material. The slot is rectangular in commercial displays with a width narrower than the body size of the whitefly – about 0.2 mm – but it must allow the full air and light transmission. Screens built to remove Bemisiatabaci still require a certain penetration rates and Frankliniellaoccidentalis cannot be omitted. We avoid the bulk of larger insects, such as moths, mosquitoes, leaf miners and aphids, and contain bee pollinators within a greenhouse.

Unwoven screens

They are constructed of rigid, unwoven polyester, polypropylene or translucent polyethylene, micro perforated. Allare rather light materials that can be spread without mechanical assistance directly over transplants or planted soil. These were primarily used as floating covers in front of the open field to strengthen early infection and to guard against early virus infection.

UV-absorbing screens

They are believed to shield crops from insect pests and mosquito-borne virus diseases, modifying the actions of insects. These results sadly are often applied to pollinators and natural enemies.

Whitefly exclusion

Whitefly-proof (50-mesh) woven displays are the most powerful mechanical barrier by far. The white fly, Bemisiatabaci is a tiny insect with a diameter of about 0.2 mm that transmits the Tylcv virus (tomato yellow sheet curl virus) and has been a limiting factor in vegetable development in the Mediterranean and near East. Although the rate of exclusion from Whitefly is usually proportional to the screen's mesh, it is not only on the basis of thoracic width and mesh scale that the insect will cross every firewall. There is an unusually strong transmission rate of whitefly because of the large range inscription samples from irregular and sliding tissues.

Double door system or SAS

Both greenhouses should be equipped with a double door or protection access device (SAS). An SAS aircraft lock into the nursery or greenhouse field stops the larvae from reaching the key planting areas quickly. The SAS even may be fitted on all sides with traps and adhesive yellow plates.

Mass trapping of insects

Color sticky bands

Any day-flying insects draw similar colors. For examples, yellow sticky tapes attract several insects and are used frequently to trap winged aphids, leafmins and adult whiteflies. Therefore, the yellow and blue cards or bands covered with adhesives are used to lure and trap flying little bug greenhouses. Blue sticky bands are especially appealing to thrips. For mass trapping the 10-40 cm long sticky bands are used for greenhouse plantings (about 100 m / ha). The bands are mounted around 1 m high between greenhouse pools 2 weeks before the transplantation; they must be maintained throughout the entire cultivation process. Yet in greenhouses where natural enemies are introduced for biological surveillance, mass trappings are not advised because various flying beneficial insects can be drawn and destroyed by yellow sticky ribbons.

Pheromone-baited traps

Pheromone water traps are widely used in Mediterranean and Near East tomato greenhouses in new, aggressive lepidopteran organisms, Tutaabsoluta (2006-12) for mass trapping. Since pheromone traps are so successful to catch man's insects, multiple traps (over 10 per ha) in a greenhouse may often eliminate enough insects to minimize dramatically the harm to the local community. The greenhouse will therefore be completely fitted with insect screens to avoid more T-males from being drawn. Completely out of the greenhouse system.

Mechanical control of diseases

Many viruses and airborne fungi and bacteria propagate from one or more extreme sources inside a field, like seed plants but also weeds occurring inside or near a seed. Elimination of plants in the greenhouse region is not easy as commercial crops are planted adjacent to private gardens and vacant crop fields. Elimination of virus reservoirs is important, particularly in young crops where there are a limited number of plants that are the focal point of infection for secondary propagation. Any disease growth near the extracted plant must be controlled. Rouging is especially successful for mechanically transmitted viruses (e.g. pepino mosaic) or by vectors. Dead leaf and flowers should be cut on a plant until it becomes a huge inoculum saprophytic base. A sharp knife will only be used to prune, with no treats remaining. Disease can only be stopped by mitigating harm to branches, stems and leaves through cultural practices. Plants from a previous crop (volunteers) create another possible infection source in a new crop. Prevention is the only option, including correct methods of processing and crop cultivation.

Mechanical weed control

The elimination of weeds is not only an essential way of removing pest and pest's diseases but also of reducing competition in nitrogen crops, light and so on. Flaming is utilizing specific propane or butane gas machinery as a fuel to establish high temperatural conditions (800–1 000 ° C). Flaming equipment generating infra-rouge radiation is produced, explicitly or indirectly. Different protective shields are needed for application between crop rows. Only annual weeds are killed; strong tolerance for grasses and repeated treatments are required. Costs are large. Black and white plastic poles are nowadays an important methods of managing weeds within the Greenhouse either locally (on rows) or over the whole Greenhouse area. Complete soil coverage can have an effect on environment conditions in the greenhouse depending on the region and the season.

MONITORING

Surveillance requires daily surveillance of the greenhouse crop and crucial hours in order to gather knowledge not just on weeds, rodents and their natural enemies but also on pathogens and their opponents. The maximum details available for an educated decision may be used to obtain visual observing signs, soil analysis or plant sections, weather records, sticky colour traps and pheromone traps. The more a crop is tracked, the more knowledge agro-business people have about what is happening in the greenhouse.

Insect monitoring using color sticky

traps

For flying insects, yellow and blue sticky cards of different sizes are suggested for surveillance in greenhouses where biological monitoring is not available. A minimum of eight sticky cards per hectare needs to be distributed in greenhouse (especially indo-climate-controlled greenhouses) throughout the different climate zones. While colored sticky bands are placed at a fixed height and must be retained during the cultivo process, sticky traps need monitoring and adjust each week, and their height has to be placed to the top of the plant canopy. Sticky color traps are certainly outstanding devices for tracking tiny flying insect vectors, but require limited experience to identify species of caught insects.

Insect monitoring using pheromone traps

For two key purposes, attractive-baited traps may be used. Firstly, they are extremely reactive and can catch disease insects that are too small to identify by other inspection methods. Furthermore, traps containing chemical attractants catch either one species or a limited number of organisms, making it harder for target pests to be detected and counted. This responsiveness and specificities allow labor saving devices in contrast to color traps that are unspecific and need a professional to do the monitoring.

Attractive traps are used for the tracking of:

• Sense insect disease activity.

• Estimate relative abundance in a specified greenhouse of a pest species.

• signals the pest species 'first appearance or peak flight operation, time for an insecticide usage or introduction of a biological barrier, or suggests the need for further scouting.

• Mass trappings of male adults are done.

The most popular application of chemicals is in traps for tracking insect populations; while the pheromones are not always substances, several publications refer to all traps with enticing bearing as pheromone traps. For supervisory purposes, chemical attractants are typically impregnated and wrapped in a rubber or plastic lure that gradually releases the active component(s) over a span of many days or weeks. The traps for certain bugs are coated in adhesive and often include the chemo. Pheromones are challenging to add in greenhouses: air flows in safe crops vary in those in the camp and thus male lepidopteran attraction to the traps may be adversely influenced by acti. The traps is more frequently used on adhesive surfaces or in funnel-shaped entrance for catching the target bug.

CHEMICAL CONTROL

Chemical regulation involves the usage of botanical or herbal, organic, inorganic chemicals that have a damaging, inhibiting or repulsive impact on natural, animal and plant-threatened species. The drawbacks of unregulated usage of chemicals became obvious after years of use. There was a tension between moral ideals of the public and the economic interests of the chemical and agri-industrial industries. Alternative methods and protection techniques were established and tougher requirements were placed into effect to accept new chemicals. However, chemical regulation also plays a significant role in the management of pesticides and pathogens in greenhouse plants. A selection of organic additives is used in a range of preparations to counter the comparatively limited number of species of rodents, pathogens and weeds. Pesticides are amongst the most effective tools of crop protection: if they are used properly they have a simple and relatively full impact. They can be used against virtually any insect and can even be used at a late stage of the production with various communities of pesticides. The zero tolerance to pests for ornamental exports and the inability to recognize cosmetic harm in other crops lead to the usage to chemical products in covered crops. Owing to the high demand of safe crops, costly pesticides and costly methods of use (such as soil drenching) will also provide economic motives to attain the high quality required for the management of pests and diseases. Therefore, greenhouse farming varies further than most other production conditions-the confined atmosphere and concentrated monoculture promote the creation of pesticides and pathogens, which necessitate chemical regulation.

Application of pesticides

Pesticides may be used as protective therapy to preserve ecosystems or as a curative remedy to kill or reduce the population of dangerous species. Absorption and transmission of the chemical into the plant is a systematic mode of operation, where the safety impact is often experienced by plant sections which are handled individually. Systemic chemicals will reak the current pathogens in the plant and remove them with the provision of curative security in the case of fungicides. Non-systemic fungicides (so-called touch pesticides) have only superficial effects, and their function is primarily preventive. The leaves, branches, root or seed-coat may be handled with pesticides. However, most goods have been produced for use on aerial plant parts. Specific formulations of pesticides have been produced for the different methods of implementation.

A variety of considerations is required when choosing the correct implementation technique for a certain pest or disease:

• product to be used

• equipment available

• type, stage, location and spread of the target organism

• kind of crop and its stage of development

• susceptibility of the crop, or pest or disease to the product

• weather conditions

• cost

Spray, dust and neck are labour-intensive but often leave a residue on the plant which continues to destroy after application. Smokes, fogs and aerosols may also be included when greenhouses are used. Such techniques blast small droplets or chemical particles through the air in order to also hit insects and other species in the field. Greenhouse solution may be spread in dry or liquid form through cultivation or space therapy.

Dry products

Dried chemicals can be used in the form of dust or as granules; they have the benefit of being used when water is a restricting factor. Dustable powders should only be used in greenhouses in some countries because the substance is prone to wind and thermal shift but due to the noticeable residue in plants, dusting is not a popular form of control over plague. Granules are applied to or blended with the soil either before or after the seeding; the active component is absorbed into soil moisture. Such materials can influence insects and nematodes. The quickly emerging seed-coating process is close to granules. Semines are intensively blended with a paste or solvent with which the pesticide was applied. When a sticky compound is used, less pesticide is needed and a dye is included as an identifying characteristic to the seeds being processed. As a consequence, the seed is soft, stable and soluble and can defend the young soil seedlings from insects and fungi, for example.

Liquid products

Fluid chemicals may be diluted with water if necessary, and for their usage a number of devices exist. In deciding the volume of spray solution required and droplet scale, the penetration across plant and product coverage on plant and flower must be taken into consideration. Depending on the product form, 100% coverage is not necessarily required: systematic pesticide may not have to protect all crops, but a maximum coverage is sufficient for use in the killing of a fairly immobile insect by a touch pesticide (most oils and solvents). The distribution of droplets is critical in order to obtain a sufficient degree of coverage, i.e. the droplet scale, whereas the amount of sprayed Liquid is less crucial. The low volume techniques enable both crop and space treatments to be implemented on the greenhouse. Spatial application involves the usage of a chemical through the soil, and it travels homogenously through space and gradually falls into the seed. Spatial treatment benefits are that less time is needed and the crop is dry (but not all agents can be administered in this way). In the other side, the crop impact appears to be small, implying that mostly flying insects are hit. This approach mostly operates preventively where fungi are used, even where little damaging happens. To order to increase the effectiveness of this procedure, airflow holes will be removed, but temperature and RH (Relative humidity) shall not be permitted to grow too high to avoid harm to crops (RH cannot be too low either).

Chemigation

Chemicals may be spread in soil or on an artificial surface in greenhouses through drainage, which limits exposure, not only to poisonous pesticides but workers and beneficial insects (natural enemies and bees). Various chemicals, including fungicides, insecticides and nematicides, may be distributed in this manner. A pesticide should be added slowly over the entire distribution era. The pesticide is only present in the solution for a short period, depending on the solvent used.

Guided or supervised control

Although IPM includes different alternate methods of regulation, the directed regulation only covers chemical activity. The aim of the directed control is to restrict the use of pesticides by deciding whether and when a control for a certain pest is needed (for optimal effect). Chemical regulation is deemed important only for controlled controls where the economic gains outweigh costs; this includes curative and not preventive pesticides. In all IPM and controlled surveillance the full eradication of the insect or disease may not be followed: it does not have to mitigate the damage, it may be economically or technologically impractical, and because of inacceptable side effects it may not be desirable. Driven control rules are often implemented in integrated control but not in the opposite direction: in IPM, directed control is not always essential.

A farmer must be willing to recognize the harmful insects and diseases of the field and determine whether to spray or not. The crop and noxious species must always be tracked throughout the growing season: the extent of infestation extrapolated at the end of the season when harvest takes place and the yield loss is established. It is not always appropriate to forecast the predicted damage and failure, particularly in the case of high-value crops, and growers typically do not obey the directed control principles. When monitoring a noxious organism, it is not only important to count numbers, but also to observe the stage of crop and plague production. The caterpillar stage of a pest insect, for instance, may be harmful for the seed, but not for adults. In comparison, one production step can be managed effectively, while another presents difficult problems. Due to the fact that the harm done by the insect or disease often depends on the crop point, the threshold amount is not constant throughout the growing season. An insect, for example, will inflict massive harm and loss of yield during germination, but a resulting infestation does not contribute to any reduction in yield. In its early phase of growth, tomato leaf miners (e.g. Liriomyzaspp. and Tutaabsoluta) are more injurious to the tomata crop than when the plant canopy is completely grown. Pest levels are, thus, complex and can be related to the plant development stage; the threshold for harm can therefore be impacted by environmental factors. However, if a single spray may potentially minimize different pest populations, the choice may be taken to implement controls to a lower probability of harm than with a pest population alone. The potential for harm is greater, because integrated monitoring allows the operation cheaper: the equilibrium between management expenses and damage done by casualties is met at a greater degree of risk, including a reduced pest community. The spraying of calendars is now commonly used with a number of offers:

• Growers that lack the requisite details on the noxious organism risk threshold.

• Growers are not often conscious of insect species and the mode of action of the chemical substance.

• Proper observation and sampling techniques, particularly for fungi, are not always possible.

• Observation period is treated as an unnecessary labor expense (even though the gross expenses are already reduced).

• In certain situations (specifically for ornamental plants) harm rates are very small (not necessarily zero), allowing spray farmers to use exclusively "natural" items.

Side-effects on beneficial organisms

Pesticides may have main and secondary effects on workers, rodents, parasitoids and other insect pathogens. Depending on sensitivity and the biological parameter affected, key results are overt or secondary. The following could be attributed to gross reproduction of beneficial organisms:

• direct contact during application

• pesticide residues

• taking up contaminated prey

• intoxication by fumigants

• contact or contamination with soil disinfectants

Secondary effects include the following:

• killing the prey/host of a beneficial organism

• killing species which produce alternative food (e.g. honeydew)

• taking up contaminated food

• directly stimulating the pest (e.g. some pyrethroids enhance reproduction in

Tetranychusurticae)

Fungicides directly influence entomopathogenic fungal biocontrol products by inhibiting sporal germination and vegetative production (mycelial growth); they are also successful in decreasing the viability and reproduction of conidias and their activities on plant surfaces.

Effects on predators

The bulk of pyrethroids and carbamates are toxic to parasitic mites. Aphidoletesaphidimyza is prone to and is often impaired by organophosphate treatment with insecticide and acaricide. The mortality rate of Coccinellides is high among virtually all compound classes other than micro-organisms and soap. Chrysopids bring harm to acaricide, mainly pyrethroids, soap and microorganisms, but they are the region influenced by the plurality of regulators for insect development (IGRs) and by organophosphate. Fungicides and herbicides are mostly harmless, but are partly toxic for coccinellides, chrysopides and biting bugs.

Effects on parasitoids

Synthetic pyrethroids and pyrethrin, irrespective of the organisms, are very dangerous to adults.

Organophosphates are very dangerous to vulnerable stages and to safe life stages of the parasitoid with few exceptions. In both the vulnerable and covered developmental stage of the parasitosis, IGRs and most the acaricides are harmless. Soap and microorganisms are harmless except for pyrethrin and neem extracts. Fungicides are typically adult parasitoids toxic. Very few herbicides damage adult guess pieces, but not guess pieces at certain stages of growth.

Pesticide resistance

The toxic influence of pesticides can be reversed by metabolizing the active ingredient into less harmful elements, decreased chemistry absorption (physiological resistance) or prevented application (consistency). Pest and disease tolerance will, of course, prove to be the greatest threat to manage pesticides. Pesticide resistant species of fungus and pests occur often in greenhouses. This trend is triggered by the reality that the greenhouse is a closed environment with the community of harvested varieties not being contaminated by the natural population outside of the region. As a result, the demand for tolerance to pesticides is considerably higher in open field crops than greenhouse crops.

Fungicide resistance

Botrytis cinereA(grey mould), Pseudoperonosporacubeinsis(powder-ful mildew of cucurbits), Didymeliabryoniae(gummy stem blight of cucurbites), and Sphaerothecafusca(powdery mildew of cucurbits) are reported to establish fungicide resistance in greenhouses.

The benzimidazole fungicides (benomyl, carbendazim and thiophanates), since they have a specific mode of action, have strong tolerance potentials to pathogens. Resistance is typically not correlated with a large loss in pathogen health. It occurs in B groups. Kinery, D. Fusarium and powdery mildews bryoniae. bryoniae. Mixtures and alternations of multi-site touch fungicides may prolong this collection prior to widespread resistance. Acute fungicide tolerance issues (e.g., iprodione, procymidone, vinclozolin) emerge when fungicides are used intensively and solely over several seasons. Isolates are mildly tolerant and just as suitable as susceptible strain where no fungicides are available. The amount of dicarboxymide treatments will not be limited to more than three per crop in greenhouses, irrespective of whether resistance occurs or not. When infection risk is strong therefore it is generally advised that such fungicides be alternated or mixed with proteins such as chlorothalonilorcaptan or biocontrol where tolerance is typically not chosen.

Ergosterol biosynthesis inhibitors (EBIs), which comprise triacole, imidazole and pyrimidine, are a category of fungicides. In comparison to the extreme sharp resistances of benzimidazoles and dicarboximides, EBI tolerance occurs in the context of sluggish pathogen changes. For eg, benzimidazoles, hydroxypyrimidines, pyrazophos and EBIs have been used to regulate powdery mildews in greenhouses for many years. Resistance occurs in S communities. Fusca, however in several countries, the alternation of fungicides tends to overcome the issue. EBI fungicides with fungicides from other classes as well as biocontrol are usually recommended to be combined or mixed. The absence of disease management in greenhouses is evidenced by a history of gray mold epidemics. In greenhouses with tolerance to benzimidazole, dithofencarb, dicarboximid and ergosterolbiosynthesis inhibitors, numerous tolerant isolates and even harsh summer conditions do not preclude the survival of fungicide-resistant isolates.

The phenylamide fungicides inhibiting the production of RNA (ribonucleic acid) were added at the period when P. cubensis was regulated mainly with defensive applications of dithiocarbamate and chlorothalonil in the late 1970s. Phycomycetes regulation.Phenylamidemetalaxyl was launched in the early 1980s and resistant strains were quickly identified. The strains immune to metalaxyl tend to be more efficient than the strains natural. Resistance in Phytophthorainfestanson tomato was also identified. Metalaxyl anti-resistance mixtures have been established to cope with phenilamide resistance.

Insecticide and acaricide resistance

The tolerance of almost all large arthropod greenhouse pests to insecticide and acaricide is well known. Biotic explanations (e.g. generation turnover, number of offspring per output and reproduction type) have a significant impact on resistance creation besides genetic and operational factors which influence the selection of resistant individuals. Bimisiatabaci has recently established resistances against a variety of traditional insecticides (neocotinoids and pyrethroides), IGRs and similar juvenile hormone (pyriproxyfen and buprofezine). In greenhouse crops, the majority of the plague plants have been selected to resist these biological parameters. The resistance to synthetic pyrethroids most widely used in greenhouse crops has grown, while Frankliniellaoeste has established resistance to most pesticide groups which leads to serious financial losses in the affected crops.

Resistance management

It is generally safer to limit a pathogens access to a range of fungicides in order to reduce the burden on the production of tolerance in pathogen species. The number of fungicide applications of the same mode of action must be reduced, especially because fungi have a number of cycles during the growing season. The insecticide tolerance control techniques for pests include different methods, categorized as: balance control (low dosing), limited number of applications), and multiple assault management (mixing application). The goal of IPM systems is to take into consideration non-target impacts on natural enemies. These are efforts to increase the compliance of desirable species for their implementation through targeting recipients for tolerance to chemicals. Until the chosen species may be introduced in pest or disease control, the degree of intensity, resilience and potential effect on the health of the resistant organisms must be assessed. In addition to being consistent with other control strategies, resistance management in IPM is another essential feature of chemical control. Tolerance control requires many approaches to reduce the likelihood of production of pesticide resistance in the target species. Resistance control

PRACTICAL RATIONAL CHEMICAL CONTROL OF GREENHOUSE PESTS AND DISEASES

A variety of methods and strategies, including protection and sanitation (as mentioned above, are essential for the control of insects and diseases. At least in the short to medium term, the usage of pesticides should remain an effective tactic, which enables farmers to continue growing a quality crop economically. It is crucial that chemicals used in IPM are made on educated assessments (ET economic thresholds) and only after the impacts on communities of pests and pathogens are taken into consideration, to ensure they are While there is a requirement for a degree of chemical regulation, pesticide use and relevant hazards should be monitored. In this case, IPM is intended to maintain pesticide applications at the minimum acceptable level, while maintaining the requisite protection Intervals before harvesting, at the lowest effective dose for the most selective products. Five crucial measures are recommended to optimize the effectiveness of the project by using pesticides; they are listed below.

Step 1: Proper identification and risk assessment of the pest's and

disease's life stage

A variety of methods and strategies, including protection and sanitation (as mentioned above, are essential for the control of insects and diseases. At least in the short to medium term, the usage of pesticides should remain an effective tactic, which enables farmers to continue growing a quality crop economically. It is crucial that chemicals used in IPM are made on educated assessments (ET economic thresholds) and only after the impacts on communities of pests and pathogens are taken into consideration, to ensure they are While there is a requirement for a degree of chemical regulation, pesticide use and relevant hazards should be monitored. In this case, IPM is intended to maintain pesticide applications at the minimum acceptable level, while maintaining the requisite protection Intervals before harvesting, at the lowest effective dose for the most selective products. Five crucial measures are recommended to optimize the effectiveness of the project by using pesticides; they are listed below.

Step 2: Choosing the proper pesticide

The right pesticide will only be picked after the grower has correctly established the weed or disease. Often, pesticides are successful against one species but are ineffective against those closely connected. In addition, one pesticide may be effective against a specific stage of growth, while another can be effective against a separate or even both stages of development. The accurate recognition of the pesticide or disease and the knowledge of its physiology and life cycle help the grower to choose the right pesticide. Growers or pesticide firms and suppliers may search for more guidance.

Step 3: Proper usage of pesticides

When the pesticide is picked, farmers must determine the amount to use. The details is on the bottle, but there are typically more than one alternative. In order to make the right choice, as much awareness about the insect or disease ecology as possible has to be learned. In insect control, considerations such as disease size and population play an important role. For example, the lowest prescribed label rate is reasonable for small worms, while the highest label rate may be needed for large worms, but persistent use of the higher rate may contribute to insect resistance. When a population of pests or pathogenes is immune, it is impossible to regulate the quantity of the pesticide. Continuous one pesticide overdosing can cause resistance to not only the pesticide, but probably other pesticides. Workers need the correct measuring instruments to guarantee that the right amount of insecticide is used. Greenhouse growers often have smaller areas to spray than farmers in their fields.

Therefore, growers could buy a series of graded cylinders labeled in milliliters and a series of high quality cups. Glass may be used, but plastic is also used to avoid breakage. Mess instruments such as graduated cylinders have graduated lips for accurate measuring and spray preparing in amounts varying from 1 to 500 liters or more. Measuring devices may ensure accurate measurement that allows successful killing, a healthy range of pesticide residues on crops, a more productive use of chemicals and money and reduction or e-commerce In the overall safety and storage of chemicals, effective measurement devices often contributes: they help prevent the spillage of volatile products. Pesticide concentrate is usually handled after filling the sprayer and preparation of diluting sprays, so special handling procedures are currently required. When treating finished sprays, however, the applicator needs to be especially vigilant with condensed content. Staff must be alert, vigilant and use all pesticides under the mark. The following issues can arise when large pesticide quantities are used:

• Crops that contain more residue than allowed by regulation that presents a health threat to customers that may prohibit the product from reaching the market.

• Unnecessary residues will be seized and burned by the authority without recourse to the grower.

• Marketing will affect potential demand for this product.

• Employees 're-entry into drug regions is extremely harmful and adds to infections, hospital costs, and growers' responsibility.

• Drugs may speed up the cycle of tolerance of the parasite or pathogen.

• Raise manufacturing costs without benefit gained.

• Phytotoxicity is more likely to exist. The level of marking must not be surpassed. If the expected outcomes are not obtained by the highest identified amount, instead alternative causes for failure must be found. The condition does not change with additional volumes of the same content. The old cliché – "If a little is fine, more is great" – will yield catastrophic effects.

Step 4: Proper timing

The chosen pesticide will be used at the correct moment and that is not a simple process. The complex and systematic method is the safest way to use chemical treatment, and a failure to treat at or close the right period is one of the key explanations for the inadequate management of pests and diseases. In light of the difficulties involved, action should be taken to help make a sound decision:

• Inspect the crop periodically and extensively, acknowledging the prevalence and any rise in occurrence of pests and diseases.

• Recognize the insect or disease, its conduct and its crop damage potential.

• If available, be mindful of economic thresholds.

• Learn the biology of the pesticide or disease in order to enable application of the pesticide at the most susceptible, weakest point. Many insect and mite levels, including the egg period, may rarely be managed. New larvae or nymphalstages are simpler to monitor and need less insecticide than mature. Pupal stadiums are not normally affected by insecticides (larvae are often difficult to control) near to this point. When societies hit a high degree, even though 95% is regulated, the remaining 5% will remain a significant amount.

Step 5: Proper application of pesticides

Proper application, including pacing, is one of the most critical measures in the management of pesticides. The first four measures are not sufficient enough to finish correctly and then not distribute the item to the goal area. There are several considerations to be taken into consideration, and specific spray systems must be carefully adjusted for the proper application of pesticides. An under dosing (not having control) or overdosing (illegal and harmful) configuration mistake may occur quickly. Application of the appropriate quantity of material is directly associated with configuration. The farmers can buy specific surgery equipment and the desired plague or disease. Could pesticide and disease varies from one piece of equipment in behaviors and actions that does not satisfy all the needs. For example, the outcomes of experiments involving greenhouse mite control equipment varied widely. Large volume sprayers also given 59% power, rotary atomizers with 67% power, and pulse-jet applicators with 8% controls. They are common, can tolerate a broad range of types of pesticides and give organizational versatility. However, large volume sprayers need a lot of effort, time consuming and poor application performance. Less than 10 percent of the active component is expected to meet the real target utilizing large volume methods. However, for large volume uses, most pesticides are numbered. The plurality of greenhouse insects and mites on the underside of the plants, as previously described, find it hard for the pest to spray, in particular for certain insecticides with physical contact (such as soaps and oil).

Storage of pesticides

This cannot be included with new pesticides. Growers will seek and purchase the necessary quantity and should not expect and store material for more than one season. Pesticides should not be kept longer than expected on the shelf. In a clean, dry location, pesticides must be processed. The safest temperatures for storage are normally room temperature (20–30 ° C), we suggest temperatures above 40 ° C. Many pesticides are susceptible to unnecessary modifications when the storage temperature dropped below zero. For precise storage information, applicators will obey the label instructions. City authority regulations surrounding storage sheds, keys and alarm signals will be observed by applicants.

Safety issues

Pesticides will cause significant issues if common sense and proper usage and disposal guidelines are not enforced. A legislative provision has been found for the pesticide name: 'the name is the law.' It is the user's obligation and legal liability to learn, comprehend, and view the directions and facts on the sticker. The definition marking will be sponsored by pesticide distributors, suppliers and their members, as well as the extension service. Failure to grasp the warning or abusing a pesticide may have adverse consequences. The mark provides details about the proper usage of its products, clothes for safety, interaction with staff, signs of contamination, disposal and other detail. The customer is advised to familiarize himself before usage with the protection and other facets of the mark.

Selected super foods

2.1. Amaranth

Botanically identified as Amaranthus, this herb was cultivated 8,000 years ago by the Aztecs and is now an ancestral herb in Peru. Amaranth's ancient past can be traced to Mexico and the Yucatan Peninsula. The term for amaranth derives from a Greek word amarantos meaning' one who does not willow or 'never willow'-as the bushy flowers of amaranth maintain their vibrancy even after harvest and desecration. Furthermore, certain varieties of ornamental amaranth do not yield spectacular flowers but instead produces colorful leaves. Amaranthusare grown now in Africa, India, China, Russia, South America and North America. Amaranth is around 6 foot tall, has large, red blood-to-purple, light-green leaves, and 60 different types, numerous of which are grown as leafy crops, cereals or ornamental plants. It is commonly recognized as pigweed (English), hanekam (Afrikan), thepe (Sesotho), mchicha (Swahili), terere (Kenya Gikuyu, Meru and Embu), doodo (Kenya Luganda), shoko (Yoruba) and lengalenga (Congolese Democratic Republic and Burundi). The amaranthleaves and the seeds are also important for human safety. Whether it is a leaf crop, cereal grain or grain flour that you prefer, despite the variety and high amounts of antioxidants and nutrients, the usage of amaranth is one of the most precious health products that you may never have heard about.

Vegetable/leafy amaranth

Amaranth crops are perhaps the most commonly consumed boiled or steamed greens in the rainy lowlands of Africa. They store millions of food supplies. The leaves and stems yield outstanding steamed or boiled vegetables, such as stew and sauce; they have a smooth feel, a slight flavor, and no trace of bitterness. As stated earlier, the nutrient rates of raw vegetable products are higher than those of cooked vegetables, although not all vegetables can be eaten. Amaranth leaves are one of the vegetables to be roasted. It should also not surpass 5 minutes when cooking the amaranth and when utilizing water, it should be used in small quantities and not discarded like most leaching nutrients. When you prepare amaranth with other foodstuffs, which take a longer cooking period, such as legumes and beef, it should be applied to the food a few minutes before the meal is finished. Therefore, amaranth leaves have a strong nutritional value, following suitable cooking methods. Cooked amaranth leaves are filled with antioxidants and are an excellent source of many nutrients, including vitamins and minerals. 100 g of cooked, leafy amaranth produces 4.6 g protein, 380 mg of calcium, 4.9 mg of magnesium, 54 mg of potassium, 42 mcg of folate, 19 mg of vitamin C, 0.25 mg of vitamin A and 228 mcg of RAE. There are very few leafy plants with high amounts of calcium, so amaranth is an absolute super food that improves bone strength and avoids osteoporosis and thereby expands the 'healthy life' into adulthood. Carotenoids and vitamin A in amaranth leaves are an essential factor in eye safety, aesthesis can avoid macular degeneration and delay or stop cataract growth. By can oxidative stress in the eyepiece, amaranth maintains the vision clear and solid. Vitamin A also plays a significant part in improving the immune system, raising the risk that pathogens may spread and their intensity.

Amaranth-based diets

Amaranth leaves come in numerous shades of dark green, reddish green and profound red and purple, but the most common variety in Africa is dark-green leafy. While the cooking amaranth is not regular ingredient, amaranth leaves and little pieces of the base, cooking oil, tomatoes, onions and salt are the main ingredients. Other ingredients that may be included depends on the culture and economic ability of the commodity include beef, small fish, groundnuts, African eggplants, green pepper, garlic or red beans. The most common usage of amaranth vegetables is starchy sauce such as steamed / boiled / stewed banana; ugali (African polenta or cornmeal mush). (Ugali)

Grain amaranth

Amaranth grain has been domesticated 6,000 to 8,000 years ago, and has a long and vivid past in Mexico. The amaranth flour is normally pale ivory on the table, but the red "puds" may also be table for a really good and spicy plant. One of the most significant features about this small grain being that it is glutenless, supplying millions of citizens that have celiac disorder or gluten allergy with a suitable wheat substitute.

At around 13-14 percent, amaranth grain easily converts the protein content of most other grains, and you can hear the protein in amaranth named 'full' because it includes lysine and an amino acid that is absent or negligible in many grains. It also includes other main proteins called albumin and globulins which are more soluble and digestible relative to prolamins in wheat. 100 g raw amaranth contains 14 g protein, 15 mg magnesium, 159 mg calcium, 4 mg vitamin C and 18 mg sugar. The high fiber amount contributes to smooth food digestion and promotes the effective absorption of minerals. Around 105% of the regular weight per meal, amaranth manganese is not included in the charts because it includes fewer carbohydrates. Amaranth produces 6 to 10 percent butter, primarily unsaturated, or around 67 percent unsaturated fatty acid, like linoleic acid, which are essential for proper nutrition. Amaranth grain is a true powerful ingredient of all the above nutrients, which can avoid a variety of chronic conditions like diabetes, heart disease, cancer and stroke.

Grain amaranth-based dishes

Grain amaranth has been used in a variety of forms by humans for milk. Since the amaranth is highly thick, it is too strong to use by itself. While it may be consumed like popcorn or flaked as oatmeal, it is better used for a lighter flavor with other grains. The grain of the bottom is used to provide staple-based foods such as porridges, soups, ugali and so on to poor people with more nutrients. Amaranth grain porridge (1 cup) and moring powder (1 cup) from moring leaves, for instance, not only offers excellent nutritional food for people with an HIV/AIDS-affected immune system but also for those using amaranth/moringa, which are capable of taking antiretroviral medicines without complications. There are over 40 amaranth goods that can be used by customers of diverse socio economic / cultural backgrounds. Amaranth grain flour is often used as a special thickener for sauces, soups, stews and even jellies; the four grains may be made from freshly grounded grains by sprouting and germinating, desiccating and frying into meal. Eaten as a snack, amaranth may have a sweet, nutty or peppery taste and texture.

HARVESTING

Stock consistency is crucial to meet potential market requirements and encourage repeat sales at harvest time. Harvest stage affects micronutrient concentration, because many (particularly carotenoids) accumulate in fruits throughout the entire cycle of growth. For most goods consistency is attained at harvest periods and degradation starts and progresses inexorably, with consistency deteriorating by senescence and death.

In order to be effective, they have to sell goods to customers who are so grateful that they purchase them again and again. Therefore, growers must constantly fulfill customer demands and desires for fresh greenhouse goods by utilizing all available technologies and know-how in order to develop, harvest, box, stock, transportation and sell their crop. Growers ought to consider the essence of the sector in which their goods are priced. They need to recognize the variables that impact commodity consistency and affect degradation after the harvest. The supply of greenhouse-grown vegetable and fruit will not only be seen to be a source of food and nutrition but should also be viewed as a healthy and good health service for households. This ensures that products must be processed, graded, packed, shipped and delivered to warehouses or markets. Sales often occur many days or weeks after harvest. Therefore suppliers, brokers, wholesalers and distributors must also be worried with preserving the consistency and reducing post-harvest losses in the chain between producers and consumers. Quality of the final product will only be accomplished if the steps in the supply chain are logically, interconnected and planned.

Packaging

Microgreens should be kept as healthy as possible without disruption to the crop after harvesting. This would be a reasonable procedure to reduce the period the substance spends at room temperature.

In a safe, cooling environment at or below 4 ° C, microgreens should be stored to reduce the microbial production. For a temperature-controlled setting the Thermometer needs to be mounted and checked periodically. Microgreens can always be handled in a manner that avoids the product harm. Stacking too many bags on top of each other may result in damages to the commodity at the bottom of the stacks, which increases the danger of a faster decay of the final product. While shelf lives that differ between species and variety, most microgreens have a shelf life with a proper handling and storing of around 5 to 10 days.

The high degree quality maintenance, maintenance and adequate handling in the package will be moved to the delivery phases. In order to reduce the possibility of pollution and microbial production, microgreens must be shipped to refrigerated regions. Although buyers will comply with specific criteria for food protection, growers can inform customers about the correct processing and storage of the plant wherever necessary. The implementation of best practices and effective crop management addressed in this factsheet will provide growers with the best outcomes for their business objectives.

Packaging is needed to bring the commodity on the market from the manufacturing center to the consumer. It has three aims:

• Protection from environmental, biochemical and biological damage through diagnosis, transport, delivery and commercialization.

• Assembly of goods for ease of handling and shipment in standard amounts (production systems, including palletization may be adopted).

• Container labeling with distinctive brand / logo advertising, stock traceability details like harvest and/or packaging date (many containers are intended to be shown on the shelf as a final show and thus include enticing lay-outs and logos as well as price barcodes). Moreover, culture concerns itself with environmental and recycling issues and requires that cans and packets will be recyclable or returnable. Around the same time products must be equipped to provide sufficient airflow during cooling and shipping and to withstand the rigors of multiple handlings in the supply chain. The box, not the commodity, has the weight of a pallet stacked and does not fail when the pallet becomes soaked in transit In general, major supermarket company sought to standardize the scale and form to minimize waste and related costs. For a few nations, it has contributed to the use of fiber board trays and recycled plastic crates or to tray shelling a 'normal footprint' with the complete size pallet. The processed microgreens can be stored at lower temperatures (at or under 4 ° C). Micro green packaging should be used in shallow containers as these containers require fast cooling and mitigate possible pathogenicity.

Labeling and certification

An appropriate marking scheme will be in effect during the manufacturing process to minimize the possibility of misidentification and infection. Extra marking, including lot identification (traceability codes), is often important to avoid a drug recall and helps proper stock rotation.

Relevant key criteria for the marking of microgreens must be included:

* common name

* allergens

* net quantity

* nutrition labelling (unless exempt)

* dealer name and address

* durable life date

* list of ingredients

* bilingual labelling (unless exempt)

CERTIFICATION OPTIONS

The credential choices available rely on the formation of the legal body applying for credential.

TRACEABILITY

Logistics technologies are shifting considerably from monitoring capacities across the whole supply chain from manufacturer to store.

• Tracking is the opportunity to trace the progress of a single object across the supply chain as it is transported across and inside organizations.

• Tracking is the opportunity to determine the sources of an object or batch of items placed anywhere and at any point in the supply chain. This monitoring may also be utilized for selling products and to insure that the commodity meets consumers on point. Traceability is challenging for most companies to enforce and robust and verifiable traceability is still a significant obstacle. But traceability is the answer to risk control and constantly requires international trading for purposes of bio-security, consumer health, physical safety as well as labels and customer defense.

• consumer preferences

• retailer profits

• wholesaler profits

• demands for safety and biosecurity from the health and agriculture authorities

• Traceability criteria for the drug to its source or contamination (criteria required even by safety and agriculture authorities)

HOW TO SELL MICROGREENS

Finding Your Local Buyers

You probably have a good list of buyers of micro-greens in your region from your research before you start the company. Or a list of possible customers who might continue shopping if there were no. Before you start hiring customers, you have a taste of your microgreen offering.

Prepare Your Message: Be able to clarify what microgreens are and why they are important additives and tastes. Have the microgreen drug ready for you: How they are used and what their health advantages are. How are you going to market them? What are the varieties? And how can you market much? The value of product suggestions assists in the marketing process. Often people don't realize what microgreens are and you may have to continue educating them from the beginning, or with some, remind them how special yours is from some.

When you start selling the microgreens on the farmers 'markets, you have plenty of time to plan the post, so that you know easily what buyers want. After a season of farmers 'sales on the street, you can speak to someone about microgreen items.

Before you go to local retailers and shops, check their premises again and see what they sell and whether it fits your purchase. See what is available, try it and talk about its size and its quality. So you should contact them with information through the commodity and its source.

Restaurants: Please notify the chef or manager if you visit a restaurant. If a manufacturer of goods, the buying team is young. In your initial touch, invite them (briefly) to show your microgreens to have a taste to leave them with samples. Get written details on your farming and how you cultivate microgreens and shoots. Build a one-page contact details file, containing all contact information, photographs, costs, varieties and quantities available. Also leave microgreen samples of each kind. If you have a restaurant, you may like to ask how they actually use it and whether they can include it in potential menu products. Ask them if they want the stuff, how much and whether things are seasonal.

Groceries: Local natural food markets and retail shops are great ways to buy your items. Contact the shop manager after your on-site analysis and send them your message and content. Offer sample monitoring. Call for a review to see if they are doing in the shop. Many of these shops support organic food activism and will be able to take a gamble on your items. Bigger, retail foodstuffs have their own delivery networks, and when you reach them, they feel like a manufacturer. But don't be discouraged, ask a shop manager how you should approach shop customers about your offer. Follow whatever guidance they offer you to reach national customers, then follow up and inquire again.

Produce Distributors: Distributors involved would most definitely ask you to complete an application, and maybe they will make their food quality / safety workers tour their farm and insure that they will produce under their specifications. You should be asking for good agricultural practices (GAP) in food health questions: is there a bathroom? Will staff be willing to wash their hands? Are contact surfaces created clean or sanitized? Which is your cooling device and should the sample be processed directly after selection and pickup? Where do you want to store the goods? How is this marked? Was the substance monitored or recorded in order to trace? During the visit to the farm you will tell the dealer how they plan to store microgreens and what the processing, marking and food health criteria are. You will have all the details about what distributors require after visiting the plant. You should decide that you are ready (or unable to) satisfy the demand for quantity, packaging or other issues.

Consider Buyer's Needs: Upon consulting the prospective client, decide whether you want to stick to what the buyers learn or seek something different. If you choose to deal in the smaller measurements or whether you like a heavy weight. What did the purchaser say? Are they going to want color? What kind of hot or medium taste? And seek to set back your own interests. It's simple to expand, but that's not what the microgreen economy desires most.

THINGS TO CONSIDERED BEFORE TAGGING PRICE TO YOUR MICROGREENS BRAND

Operating costs

The measurement and careful control of production costs will become a standard activity in order to insure that you operate a productive and sustainable company. Both expenses (fixed and variable) must be taken into consideration and the income targets set.

Fixed costs

(expenses that do not change month to month)

-- corporation may vary in the fixed costs, but all costs must be taken into consideration. Since such costs are overhead or indirect manufacturing costs, manufacturers that fail to focus on the ultimate price of the goods.

Several explanations of fixed costs are as follows:

• management and sales salaries

• insurances (liability, property, crop etc.)

• facility or land costs (mortgages, leases, property

taxes, etc.)

• repair and maintenance costs

• marketing (examples, website and social media

expenses)

• yearly accounting and administrative fees

• debt interest payments

Variable costs

(expenses that change month to month)

Usually, these costs are influenced by the amount of labor, supplies and varied costs encountered when manufacturing the commodity.

Here are some examples of variable costs:

• seed (cost varies by species)

• planting medium

• planting materials (examples, trays, paper towel, labels)

• packaging (examples, plastic bags, clamshells)

• labels

• shipping costs

• marketing (examples, price lists, advertising)

• labour (examples, grower, processor, delivery)

• utilities (heat, water, power)

Profit goals

(margin on top of cost of production)

It is necessary to find a balance between income expectations and the local market. Setting such big expectations produces an ambitious premium that customers will not be able to pay.

Financial forecast

As much as the place will cost, you should check at 'benchmarks' prices on your business. If, in your study, you find microgreens for sale, how far have they been sold? Have they been of the same consistency or depth as yours? How much do producers, small organic farms or grocery stores cost? Wholesale prices will be clear on the pages of other retailers. Gain an overview into the size, then analyze the costs: are you meeting the unit costs? You're earning money? Is it worth the job you're doing? If the answers are still open, set your prices and hold your gun with the buyers.

HOW TO SET UP EFFICIENT MARKETING AND SALES FUNNEL TO GET YOUR PRODUCT ON SHELVES

What is Marketing?

Continuous access to advertisements and personal selling causes us to connect and sell, or to believe that marketing efforts begin until goods and services are created. While marketing definitely involves sales and ads, it involves a lot more. Marketing often entails identification of market desires and the obtaining of knowledge required to create and deliver products or services that are compatible with purchasing requirements, and the establishment and management of relationships with consumers and suppliers.

Point of difference Selling Marketing

Starting point	Factory	Marketplace
Focus	Existing products	Customer needs
Means	Selling and promoting	Integrated marketing

End	Profits through volume	Profits through satisfaction

This famous quotation can better explain the distinction between selling and marketing: 'Don't tell me how nice your stuff is, but tell me just how happy it would make me.'

The American Marketing Association, the representative body of academic and skilled marketers, describes marketing as: Marketing is the mechanism for preparation, selling, promotion and delivery of concepts, products and services in order to create transactions that meet individual and corporate goals. Clearly put: Advertising is a reward for providing consumer loyalty.

Many current concepts such as marketing is the method of establishing and addressing exchanges and 'marketing is the mechanism through which exchanges between individuals and social classes' affirm the idea of trade as a core part of marketing. The core of marketing is the cycle of trade in which two or more parties trust one another to satisfy perceived needs. Citizens sell physical goods for capital in certain markets. Among some, they deal among intangible services. Marketing transaction does not only take place between two individuals, but much of the time between two or three groups, one or more of whom takes on the position of buyer and one or more, the position of seller. There are rising situations in the industry, i.e.,

1) Buyers outnumber sellers

2) Any individual buyer is weaker than any individual seller economically, but

3) The total economic power of even a fraction of the buyers is enough to assure the existence of, or to put out of business, most sellers or groups of sellers, and

4) Therefore, the sellers bid to control the greatest number of customers they want ahead of the offerings of other sellers (competitors). Finally and interesting,

5) In an attempt to satisfy demand to gain the greatest number of customers sellers are often motivated by an attitudes to adjust with time such that they become more competitive for more consumers. The extended scope of marketing operations includes all operational functions. This means that the campaign initiative meets the broader business plan which is carried out pursuant to best principles that successfully represents both society's which organizational needs. The definition often defines the marketing variables –

commodity, quality, advertisement and distribution – that combine to please clients. Furthermore, it appears that the company starts with the definition and review of the customer markets it must eventually encounter via its manufacturing and marketing activities. The importance on the development and continuity of ties is compatible with the company's concentration on long-term, mutually rewarding revenue, acquisitions and other relationships with clients and suppliers. Finally, it acknowledges that communications principles and strategies are accessible to not - for-profit entities, profit-oriented companies, company associations and business agencies, domestic and multinational associations and to customer and other organizations.

MARKETING CONCEPT

Needs, Wants and Demands

The fundamental concept behind ads is that of human needs. A requirement is astatic poverty. It's part of the human composition. Human beings have multiple desires, including bodily needs, social needs, emotional needs, etc. Wish are the type taken by the needs that the community and identity of one is formed. Therefore, both internal and external influences form the desires. Wants are described in terms of artifacts that meet requirements. For one, thirst is a need. An individual may find a variety of possibilities to quench this thirst – drink water or a soft drink or a fruit juice. Such items (which reflect the different choices an individual wants to meet) form the list of possible goals. By more items that generate curiosity and appetite, retailers seek to make more opportunities, that is, more goods to fulfill consumer desires. Nearly infinite citizens want only small money. They choose to pick items that please their money the most. If you purchase money (money), a need is a requirement.

Products

A commodity is something to meet a desire or wish that can be sold to a customer. Citizens serve their desires and want things. While a physical object is implied by the term, the product definition is not restricted to physical artifacts. Marketers also use the words goods and services to differentiate between real and intangible items. Such products and services can be vehicles, food, machines, locations, people and even ideas. Customers determine which entertainers to watch on TV, which places to visit during their vacation, which solutions to carry on their issues, etc. The word commodity thus includes tangible products, facilities and a number of other automobiles that may fulfill the desires and wishes of our consumers. When the word 'good' often does not seem to be acceptable, alternative words such as business offering are used to accommodate them.

Value and Satisfaction

When consumers have too many options to choose from to meet particular criteria, how will they select from so many products? We buy based on their expectations of the worth of a commodity. Customer loyalty is the driving principle. A consumer measures each product's capacity to satisfy its needs. He / She might classifies the items from the most rewarding to the least satisfactory. Of example, the perfect solution provides all the benefits at zero expense, but there is no such device. Nevertheless, the buyer can consider a current product based on the closeness of the perfect product and eventually choose a product that better benefits the rupee – the greatest value.

Exchange, Transactions and Relationships

Marketing takes place as individuals want to meet their desires and choose to exchange. Return is the process of receiving something from another by giving it in return. When it is just one of the many ways individuals can accomplish a desired object, a culture can generate much more than for some alternate method. Several requirements must be fulfilled in order for a trade to take effect. Obviously there must be at least two sides, one with a preference for the other. One party must also want to negotiate with the other party and each party must be free to accept an invitation from the other. Each group will eventually be able to connect and perform.

Such requirements clearly provide for trade. If the swap takes place necessarily depends on how the sides enter an understanding. Whether they accept, we will assume that both have been better served or not worse off through the trade. After everything, all was able to refuse the bid or approve it. In this context, trade produces value even like value is produced by output. It offers consumers with more business options. A purchase is the calculating communication tool. This requires a swap in principles between two sides. A monetary exchange includes the gain on investment for selling products and services, while a commercial deal implies the exchanging of goods and services for certain goods and services. The selling of sales is part of the broader concept of ties. Marketing is moving from attempting to optimize the benefit on each particular deal to optimizing mutually beneficial ties. It is focused on the premise that successful deals would occur if strong relationships are formed.

Markets

The sale principle refers to the business definition. A consumer is the present and prospective customers of a commodity. It can operate as a marketplace in a physical world or as a virtual ecosystem (on the Internet platform). Understand the essence of a business, consider a wild community with four men alone: a peasant, fishermen, a potter and a hunter.

Formulation of marketing strategy

The most extensive, long-term marketing practice is plan formulation. Complex and subtle alignment with other organizational functions is important at this stage. All practical approaches ought to work within an organizational plan. Because messaging works with consumers and the business climate, this is an early aspect of the overall campaign phase. When performed right, the brand approach cannot be isolated from the business plan. The marketing approach is to deal with business conditions (a particular category or subset of the business) such that the product / service product can be priced soundly and provides simple 'value guarantees' to the customer that are distinguishable from competition's products and thereby prepare the organization well for future competitive responses.

Marketing Planning

Marketing preparation requires 2-5 year term priorities and goals, and it is far from day-to-day execution operation. Due to their wider and long-term effect, proposals are typically produced by a mix of senior management and personnel specialists. When the experts take over the operation, they lack the determination and experience of the line managers responsible for executing the program. Perhaps more critical than the actual design paper is the preparation phase. A practical, informative, coherent document is created and contributes to essential organization's own learning and growth.

Marketing Programming, Allocating and Budgeting

This aspect of the marketing cycle is very comprehensive and usually focuses on the one-year period. Just one element of the marketing combination such as the sale of one or more commodity or both elements of a particular product or industry may apply to programs. To some degree, the option is dictated by the essence of the organization of the product. The more structured the company (e.g. the separation of marketing activities such as advertisement, distribution, etc.) is, the more probable it is that all goods and customers are combined with one dimension. Organizations coordinating goods and services tend to develop strategies for each commodity as well. Allocating is a necessary function, because scarcer tools, such as advertising budgets or marketing activities, are never sufficient to meet the 'needs' of all items, customers and initiatives. Marketing in several cases determines what is not to be: what is not to be marketed, and goods are not to be made, etc. Assignment is the systematic method of deciding what to do and not do and how many to accomplish. Since marketers appear to be ambitious, they frequently underestimate the commitment required to accomplish a target. Allocation needs the deep skepticism to differentiate between explicitly possible and optimistic. The budgeting represents activities and expenditures in a variety of predictive modeling forecasts, which are relevant both in and outside of the marketing method. The budgets typically provide financial forms that are used to predict cash flows and requirements through monitoring and funding functions. In addition, these often provide unit revenue estimates used by production preparation staff to 'complete the facility' or to run a business. If the forecasts are too weak, consumer expectations are fulfilled and profits are missed. If the projections are too small, the power is unused and the costs greatly exceed the estimates.

Marketing Implementation

The design of plans, campaign preparation and preparing, distribution and budgeting both contribute to campaign. That is the development process that provides the final effects in part. The strongest methods, initiatives and projects may be destroyed by bad execution. The overarching aim of all before deployment is to achieve outstanding results. Deployment involves various things to different individuals in the enterprise. As a retailer, it means going through all phases of the selling process, while it might involve reorganizing the whole sales force to the sales manager. Due to the relatively short period in which most executing tasks take place, tracking and auditing is usually easier than for longer-term policies and plans. The effects are seen by individuals who do stuff – purchasing, selling, teaching, reorganizing, etc. In contrast with most other functional fields, marketing execution is special, as the primary emphasis of marketing is beyond the business. Marketing execution is therefore based on targets, consumers, dealers, suppliers and centers of pressures (which affect buying decisions – but they do not specify). But promotion often includes interacting with certain functionalities in order to obtain popularity and to improve teamwork. Project managers, for example, will execute their strategies and projects in certain functional fields by project growth, distribution, operation and logistics staff.

Marketing means a very fascinating conflict between the mechanisms developed by the organization to direct marketing operations and the skills of marketing managers. Which occurs in most companies is that over time the systems are rigid and brittle to changing market demands, which direct all the businesses they don't want to touch! It is only through the timely involvement of the advertisers that successful marketing activities succeed from utilizing their unique ability to 'subvert the company to the standard.'

Monitoring and Auditing

One justification for designing schedules, strategies and budgets is for a collection of targets or criteria for evaluating efficiency. Two parts are usually used in brand evaluations. The first is a success evaluation toward subjective criteria. The second component of a systematic audit discusses the business procedures and other non-quantifiable factors. Since marketing is a combination of art and technology, quantitative and qualitative, and includes too many immersive variables, it is impossible to inspect.

The report illustrates a host of relevant subjects:

1. Who is to perform the audit? Can designers, programmers and executors work without any prejudice? If not, who understands the process well to carry out the audit? Can experts like advisors be interested and to what extent?

2. So many occasions will the report be conducted? Will it be routine or just on those significant points?

3. How comprehensive will the report be? Does it include anything or only certain facets of marketing? Although the investigation normally refers to an operation being performed on such days, the reporting typically refers to a routine analysis process. It more often applies to an analysis of external data rather than internal operations. It is therefore an essential aspect of the overall communication cycle as it constantly tracks the success of initiatives and services.

Analysis and Research

Each judgment on marketing should be focused on close consideration and testing. The study and evaluation must not be abstract, but should be careful and the scale of the decision taken. Nothing substitutes common sense and good judgment, while systematic study and research are essential. The marketer's knowledge includes a number of effective analytical instruments and rapid development of support systems for decision-making, mathematics and statistics and other disciplines including psychology and sociology means that the variety and strength of the instruments continue to grow. Both methods must be applied to the judgment cautiously and intelligently. It is indeed a fine line between healthy skepticism and careless misuse of valuable devices. The correctly used analytical technique will significantly boost marketing decision-making. Marketing campaigns and estimates are typically one of the basic organizational records of the enterprise. For example, the plan and budget revenue projections are the production schedule for the production feature. Those, in effect, become the training plans for the human resources system which suggest that the financial structure will fund job capital. If the funding of a large inventory and receivable rates cannot be covered the revenue estimate, development plan and personnel system must be raising. In most organizations, these lateral relations have to be a big effort. The need for teamwork is really strong and the tension is always big. Similar reward systems often promote specific types of behavior. Risk aversion and vigilance for rewards vary. The company will establish formal and informal forms of encouraging good, transparent lateral ties.

Schematic of Marketing Process

A scheme outlining an overarching phase of creation of marketing strategies. As shown, five key fields of research (5 Cs) are part of marketing decisions – consumers, businesses, rivals, staff and circumstances. In each of these fields, the concerns to be answered are:

Customer needs - What needs do we seek to satisfy?

Company skills - What special competencies do we possess to meet those needs?

Competition - Who competes with us in meeting these needs?

Collaborators - Who should we enlist to help us and how do we motivate them?

Context - Which (say, economic, technical or legal) environmental variables restrict what is feasible?

This first contributes to the identification of the target audience and the optimal location and the targeting strategy. This helps in the development and maintenance of consumers that improve profits for the business. Under this system, the value generation takes place by defining the section of the target, determining the placement of the product and service and creating the correct goods, place (distribution) and promotion for the chosen market. Pricing aims to maximize revenue for both the business and the consumer. Money obtained from the acquisition and maintenance of consumers for the good of the business.

Environmental Scanning and Environmental Management

Marketers ought to track important patterns and changes in the market world closely and constantly. The method of gathering knowledge on the global marketing climate is environmental screening to detect and understand emerging patterns. The aim of this intervention is to examine the evidence gathered to assess if the observed patterns constitute opportunities for and/or risks for the business. This decision, in effect, helps a corporation to decide the appropriate approach to a specific ecological shift. Environmental management is an attempt to accomplish corporate goals by anticipating and affecting the strategic, political, environmental, technical and social-cultural climate of the enterprise. International industry growth has made environmental screening and resource monitoring difficult. These systems will also have to follow international events, economic conditions and cultural forces elsewhere in the world. While the business climate may extend beyond the boundaries of the organization and the product strategy, efficient marketers constantly seek to anticipate their effect on marketing decisions and change their situation as much as possible.

The Competitive Environment

To order to attract consumers, the open interaction on the market with companies produces a dynamic atmosphere. Through particular company's strategic choices affect customer reactions on the market. They often influence rivals 'marketing strategies. Consequently, decision-makers will continuously track the marketing practices of their rivals – goods, platforms, costs and promotions. Things such as power, water and cooking gas embrace large-scale control by municipal bodies. Some businesses, such as pharmacy suppliers, also receive temporary patent monopoly. Currently, advertisers face three forms of rivalry. Its most obvious rivalry among advertisers with similar goods arises as an insurance firm competes with other insurance companies. The second form of rivalry includes goods where consumers will substitute each other. The no-frills, low-cost carriers contend with rail and luxury bus systems in the travel demand for replacement products directly. The last kind of rivalry takes place between all other companies vying for sales from customers. Current economic theory finds trade to be a war between firms in a particular market and businesses replacing products and services. However, advertisers have to acknowledge the fact that both businesses contend for a small amount of disposable purchasing capital. As a competitive landscape frequently dictates a product's effectiveness or failure, advertisers must continuously evaluate the marketing tactics of their rivals. A business will track closely emerging consumer developments, including technical innovations, price deflation, unique sales and other strategic deviations, and modifications to combat such improvements may be needed in the company's marketing mix. Marketers of each organization must establish an appropriate approach to cope with their business climate. In certain parts around the planet, one business can operate in a wide variety around markets. Another may be concentrated in specific market categories, such as those based on geographical, age and income profiles of consumers. To assess business policy, three questions need to be answered:

(1) Should we compete?

The solution to these questions is focused on the finances, goals and aspirations of the business for the benefit opportunity of the sector. An organization may opt not to acquire or proceed to run a future profitable product that does not conflict with its finances, goals or expectations of income.

(2) If so, in what markets should we compete?

The response needs marketers to consider their finite capital (sales workers, promotional budgets, product production capacities, etc.). They will take accountability for the best-chance use of this capital.

(3) How should we compete?

This implies that marketers will make product, size, distribution and promotional choices to provide their business with a competitive advantage on the market. Companies may invest in a broad variety of statements, including product content, price and customer support. Of example, a company may achieve competitive leverage by better consumer support, whereas other competitors may provide cheap prices. Many businesses utilize time as a strategic economic tool by enhanced foreign competitiveness and fast evolving technologies. A business approach is aimed at producing and selling products and services quicker than rivals. A versatile and time-based approach helps the business to improve product efficiency, lower prices, adapt to competition and increase the range of its offerings to reach different areas of the market and improve consumer loyalty.

The Political-Legal Environment

By already knowing the regulations, no-one can try to play a new game; certain businesses have dramatically restricted awareness of the political-legal climate of marketing – the laws and their definitions that allow corporations to work in such economic constraints and to safeguard customers. Ignorance of or refusal to comply with the rules, legislation and legislation will lead to penalties, prejudicial adverse coverage and potentially substantial litigation lawsuits. Companies need to be extremely cautious to consider the regulatory basis around their commercial decisions. Many of the laws and legislation influence such actions, which are explicitly defined by a multitude of various bodies, and are being applied in a contradictory manner. Such standards and bans influence all facets of decision taking on marketing — design, marking, manufacturing, distribution, advertisement and promotion of products and services. Many large corporations provide in-house legal resources to cope with the big, dynamic and evolving political-financial environment; small businesses also receive qualified guidance from legal experts. However, all traders should be informed of the key regulations which influence their activities. Other possible business-related problems from the political and legal environment include:

The national foreign policy can dominate the international business decisions of the local firms

Government political philosophy will influence foreign brands who want to join a market

The rivals working closely with the government will help to create trade barriers for a business

Global trade organizations will impose trade barriers if their rules and guidelines are not complied with

A host country may place anti-dumping duties on a foreign company and a decision like this could be controlled by local companies lobbying government

Copyright infringements, trademark and intellectual property rights violations

Direct comparative advertisements may not be allowed in few countries

Use of children is advertising and advertising to children are banned in certain countries

Price regulations preempt any pricing strategy of a firm

A detailed displaying of the ingredients in product labels is mandatory in most countries

The channel members are given the additional responsibility of verifying the eligibility of the prospective buyers for certain products

Use of certain raw materials or methods of manufacturing are prohibited in certain countries

Industry watch dogs and advocacy advocates are not in favor of any deceptive advertising practice Each of the above problems has significant repercussions for the marketer in decision-making regarding the marketing process. Ignorance of the law is no excuse and breach of the law is a felony.

The Economic Environment

The general economy's wellbeing determines how many customers invest and purchase. This arrangement often operates in the opposite direction. Market spending plays an animating function in the stability of the economy. In addition, consumer purchasing consistently accounts for nearly two thirds of the overall economic operation. Since all marketing strategies are intended to meet customers 'needs, advertisers will consider how economic conditions affect customer purchasing decisions. The economic world of marketing includes factors that affect the buying power of customers and marketing strategies. They represent the stage of the economic cycle, inflation, jobs, supply of services and wages. The economy of a country has traditionally continued to adopt the cyclical trend of our periods of growth, decline, downturn and regeneration. In-point of the sales cycle, customer buying varies and advertisers will change their tactics accordingly. Market buying in periods of growth holds pace. Marketers respond by widening product ranges, growing sales campaigns and rising delivery to boost market share and reduce costs so as to improve their profit margins. During recessions, customers frequently shift their buying habits to prioritize inexpensive, low-priced, practical goods. During these days, advertisers will take into consideration lower price costs, remove unwanted goods, boost customer satisfaction and raise advertising expenditure to generate demand. In a crisis, consumer consumption dropped to the lowest level. In the economic recovery process, the economy recovers from the crisis and the buying power of customers is rising. Although the potential of customers to purchase rises, treatment also reduces their desire to buy. You should invest rather than spend or purchase on cash. As other economic elements, sales cycles are dynamic processes that appear to threaten marketers 'influence. Success relies on versatile strategies that can be adjusted across various markets cycle periods to satisfy customer demand. Inflation devalues capital by rising goods it will purchase by continuously growing costs. Purchases would be less serious if wages were to be aligned with increasing rates, but mostly not. Inflation reduces advertisers 'expense such as salary and raw material costs, and therefore increased rates may have a detrimental effect on revenue. Inflation makes consumers conscious of costs, especially during high inflation times. This effect will lead to three potential consequences, all of which are essential to marketers. (1) Customers may prefer to shop now, anticipating the demand rises eventually, (2) can choose to change shopping habits and (3) delay such transactions.

Unemployment is characterized as the share of people in the economy who have no jobs and are engaged in their quest for work. It increases through recessions and falls in the economic cycle's recovery and growth. Unemployment influences ads, including inflation, by shifts in customer behavior. Consumers may opt to save rather than spend. Another significant determinant of the economic climate of marketing is employment, as it affect customer buying ability. Marketers will predict consumer demand by looking at income figures and patterns and create strategies to reach particular customer segments. To advertisers, an uptick in revenue will boost total revenues. Yet they are more involved in the discretionary income, the amount of money that citizens expend on necessities. Consumers 'discretionary income ranges greatly based on demographic factors such as age, and education rates. Brisk demand can lead to orders that exceed production ability or exceed the response time needed for preparing a production line. A shortage of raw materials, component parts and or labour can often represent a lack of resources. Notwithstanding the cause, the scarcity causes advertisers to reorient their strategy. One response is demarketing, a mechanism that lowers customer appetite for a commodity that the business can fairly produce. A supply scarcity poses a complex range of threats to advertisers. This could be appropriate to distribute restricted resources that are a separate practice from the conventional goal of selling to increase sales range.

The Technological Environment/ The industrial world reflects the application of research, creativity and engineering developments to marketing. New technology contributes to innovative consumer goods and services, enhances similar items, increases customer satisfaction, and often lowers costs by modern, cost-efficient manufacturing and delivery processes. Technology can easily replace products, but it can open up fresh marketing possibilities almost as rapidly. The marketing world is revolutionizing technologies. Technological advances not only produce innovative goods, but also build whole new sectors. The Web recently changed the way businesses collaborate with different partners to increase consumer satisfaction. Technology can sometimes tackle social and environmental issues through offering inexpensive, non-polluting, energy-conserving, and sustainable goods, as well as promoting equality among customers through offering fair access and ability. The business has a significant strategic edge in innovative uses of emerging technology. Marketers that track and effectively utilize emerging technologies will therefore improve customer support.

The Social-Cultural Environment

The social and cultural marketing system explains the interaction between marketing and community and its history. Marketers will remain alert to rising social standards and structural trends such as population increases and improvements in aging distribution. Such shifts influence the responses of customers to specific goods and marketing strategies. The social and cultural backdrop also has a more profound effect on foreign marketing decision-making than on the domestic environment. Learning regarding cultural and social disparities between countries is an important precursor for the performance of a business abroad. Marketing campaigns in one world frequently struggle when implemented explicitly in other nations. In certain instances, retailers are creating packets and adapting goods and promotional ads to match the needs and desires of various communities. Evolving societal norms have contributed to consumerism, an urban common movement that supports and preserves consumers through demands on industry in civil, moral and economic terms. Consumerism also supports market freedoms, for example:

1. The right to choose freely – Consumers would be able to select from a range of goods and services

2. The right to be informed – Sufficient awareness and quality knowledge should be accessible to customers to make informed purchasing decisions

3. The right to be heard – Consumers, suppliers, retailers, customer services and the courts, will be permitted to submit valid allegations to the relevant parties.

4. The right to be safe – Consumers should be confident of no harm to everyday usage incurred by the products and services they buy. Product architecture will enable ordinary customers to use them safely. The social / cultural climate is growing in complexity and significance for marketing decisions at home and abroad. There is no marketer actually willing to implement a marketing judgment by taking into consideration society's expectations, beliefs, history and demographics. The relentless stream of media feedback allows campaign executives to concentrate on certain problems rather than only use traditional communication methods.

BRANDING

Goods are produced in the factory, but products are made in the head. Each business organization wants an image to market itself. A 'name' is a distinctive organizational image reflecting the make-up, meaning or heritage of the goods. This is necessary to pick a brand name for a company or a commodity. If the business is a sole proprietor, a limited partnership or some organization, it wants a name of its own to distribute or advertise its goods and services to allow effective networking and successful selling and marketing performance. A brand is not a mark or a strap sequence, it is more important than that. They build and revitalize products through their portrayal and a dream and a collection of values. Through strong messaging and effective networking, one company will flourish. Every all such products or services will be a common word, whether it is young or elderly, as it performs. It is vital that each company will be well marketed in order to advertise and to sell. Through organizations such as Google and SAS Institute, workers are their first client. The loyalty of the consumer is without a doubt a key factor in the performance of the enterprise. Customer penetration and create a reputation is a vital aspect of market performance. Quality is reflected in the willingness to see clearly how lifelong consumers will be generated for a lifetime. When your consumers are worried about you, the lenders can do so. Without selling strategies, a corporation is most likely to struggle. When reaching the market, each business will raise concerns about its own organization about the sale of its goods or services. Questions such as "How do I get customers to purchase my product? "And" What's the feature we have some people don't have? "These issues may also help businesses or organizations accomplish what they desire by concentrating on the desires of the target audiences and, meanwhile, having a need to pursue the latest pattern. Nowadays the solution to this problem is always really valued by businesses, but they do recognize that consumers are not the only thing they need to do. Consumers don't hold to those goods for a lifetime in today's industrialized environment. That is basically because they continually adjust the items they select to increase their interaction with various labels during the major selling cycle. The advertisement of the market and the increasing sense of individuality have shaped customers who can share goods, items or services as long as they feel the need to. Every business, whether large or small, does its hardest to create brand loyalty in this customer climate. Brand loyalty is the important element in sustaining the willingness of customers to purchase a particular item over and again from specific dealers.

The Web has been a basic necessity as it provides more opportunities to all over the globe. The Internet is now open to all; workers can monitor communications and carry out their jobs effectively, and most notably, businesspeople can handle their job even though they come from other nations. Everybody believes the Internet produces a neo-economy and some analysis suggests that the main growth driver of e-commerce would be independent, medium or big enterprises.

The creation of encounters with the actual product / service specifically linked to its application and the impact of advertisement, architecture and media analysis produce brand awareness and other reactions. For an ideal business environment, businesses must make an attempt to outdo themselves for order to succeed on a market. Currently, numerous corporations are struggling to win without understanding the value of the competition. A brand also includes a specific name, icons, color schemes, colors and sounds.

Online Marketing

The Internet has been an important part of life for everyone. Some claim they couldn't live without the internet. It's only that the Internet has offered us too much comfort. With the existing of internet, one can easily get their job done easily with all sorts of research on the searching engine even though they are overseas and it is impossible to hand in the work to the lecturer or employer. There are incredible amounts of users who access the Internet. In average, 75% of the population of the United States is online and figures are growing every day. Digital marketing, sometimes referred to as online marketing, digital marketing, e-marketing and web marketing. This is a device, process or technique to offer the public a firm identity. Today's new mobile generation, app subscribers are 1.75 billion. Organizations adopting the phenomenon will be mindful that marketing or promoting electronic goods and services offers additional advantages, profits and income to the business. It is because someone who owns a mobile will access the internet anywhere, wherever they choose. However, with advanced technologies today, businesses could easily meet a worldwide audience via internet marketing without any doubts. Digital marketing allows consumers to do anything without leaving anywhere. Digital marketing is an operation or method that assists a business in establishing its brand, image, credibility and identity through the usage of different platforms and technologies on the Web. However, internet networking often acts as a communication technique for advertising social network goods and services such as Facebook, Twitter and YouTube. Look at us, who doesn't have a Twitter page or Facebook? About everyone we meet has at least one account. According to Fast Business, some 93% of advertisers utilize social media to advertise their name, goods or businesses. Social media is a perfect communication tool to improve company productivity and the partnership between employees. The presence of an innovative, entertaining or appealing website can boost the likelihood of consumer viewing. This would also contribute to higher revenue for the business that advertises or sell its goods through social media. Networking extends our horizons and worldviews, opens us to other cultures, tests our viewpoint and thought and may open up fresh possibilities beyond excitement. Ask every founder or chief to tell us that professional networking is one of the main keys to your career success. Networking is without question a valuable work experience for company and career opportunities, especially between entrepreneurs and brokers. In addition, social networking platforms provide up-to-date details. At the same time, the social network has an overwhelming influence because people invest a lot of time on the Internet, post their impressions on their own social networking page and have a major effect on the business.

How Brands Establish Brand Loyalty.

"The winning brands would be those who identify and depend on new consumers and constantly execute on it." "Brands need to hear what people want and mean and react to them. Brands inaccessible to the public would be revealed and their image tarnished. There are two definitions of brand loyalty which imply "inertial" brand loyalty as a result of a lag of knowledge of the brand and also "cost-based" brand loyalty as a result of interim utility impact. Confidence comes first to build brand loyalty (Tate, 2013). Adapting to change can be challenging for companies, and brand loyalty can only be accomplished after the customer has built confidence in the company. Today, economies are getting more crowded and efficient. To countering improved competition, marketers require a distinct and special idea that is squarely on their customers 'minds. If there is client interest, consumer satisfaction happens. The connection between consumer satisfaction and brand loyalty is also directly proportionate.

Real loyalty is typically seen by buybacks and improved purchases, high-quality goods and services that are essential to brand loyalty, however the bar has been lifted. Today, only products with a strong emotional connection with customers are loyal. What successful marketers have in common is the willingness, every day across all nations, to offer reliable, meaningful and distinct commitments.

How to brand New Products through Online Advertising in New Economy?

The first step is to grasp the commodity itself and to love it. When we have interpreted our goods right, we as sales personnel will reassure the target audiences by offering ads or direct selling by planning a good argument for their target group to purchase from us rather than the competition. Customers will also buy digitally on a mobile. New companies that use online ads to sell their latest goods will enter foreign markets and touch citizens worldwide. Internet ads gives customers fantastic incentives to buy the company as they had always wished to explore. Today, every client needs ease and not trouble in to something or doing stuff. Promotion Products, as we will see now, is incredibly relevant because they're operating for an everyday job or an ecommerce. Branding is the strongest approach for the promotion or networking with brands functions to have a positive effect for customers and any client can know and recognize the identities of each brand.

Not to mention sales and ads. Growing product must be accurately written and clarified as marketed, so that clients recognize and trust and obtain a positive reputation for that brand. The brand of such items is a household name, and is used and checked by several customers. Under this scenario, the company will have client loyalty standards.

How does an organization create a customer?

In fact, "making" involves the recognition of requirements in the market, the assessment of those requirements the company will gain and the production of a product to turn prospective consumers to customers. Marketing managers are accountable for the bulk of actions required in order to build the organization's customers.

- Identifying customer needs.
- Designing goods and services that meet those needs.
- Communication information about those goods and services to prospective buyers.
- render the products and services accessible to the consumers at times and locations.

- Pricing of products and services to represent prices, competitiveness and consumer buying capacities.
- Providing the correct support and reporting after payment to ensure consumer loyalty.

For an organization to truly globalize and thrive, however, it must do something to build a brand that will draw customers with the terms or the slogans that are behind it. Not only does the creation of a company not a requirement to reduce the ability to create fresh products, but one that can be done in the near term for the retailer to market. In order to boost revenue, the facilities provided to customers are of considerable significance. It offers local and foreign advertisers a strategic advantage on its competitors. Branding is so important to every company that it will boost its profits at a greater degree, beyond a strong marketing campaign. However, further ads and research of one company would give an edge to the brand itself. If and when customers consider it interesting, the brand value of the company will be moved to the next point. Branding is a crucial term for a good company. With the well known brand mark, a decent company will quickly be recognized and remembered. Thanks to this evidence, it strongly shows that effective multinational or local companies cannot be a simple job to manage the goods of various brands. That is where the difficulty resides, because without great challenges it will not be important for us to develop our perception of others in order to be effective in business today and in the future.

CONCLUSION

Microgreens are tasty and can be blended into the diet in a broad variety of ways.

They are still really healthy in general and may also raising the chance of other diseases.

Since it is simple to develop at home, it is especially economical to raise intake of nutrients without having to buy huge numbers of vegetables.

Microgreens seem to have a major nutritional value. A research by the USDA's Agricultural Research Service (ARS) showed that nearly all tiny greens produced around 5 times more nutrients than those present in the mature leaves of the same plants at equivalent weight. The investigators have tested essential vitamins and carotenoids in 25 commonly grown microgreen species, including red chops, cilantro, garnet amaranth and green daikon radiation, including vitamins C, E (tocopherols), K and beta carotene.

They noticed that the amount of nutrients differed greatly. For examples, the total amount of vitamin C varied from 20 mg to 147 mg per 100 grams of seed leaves. Beta-carotene, lutein, zeaxanthin and violet (orange pigment) varied from roughly 0.6 mg to 12.2 mg per 100 grams of cotyledon fresh weight. They also stated that red cod microgreens had the lowest of vitamin C, and that green daikon dramatically produced the most vitamin E. (The authors noted that an apple's weight was 100-150 grams for comparison) Nutrient quality may therefore differ considerably based on where the greens are planted, processed and the soil they are using.

Do Not Go Yet; One Last Thing To Do
If you enjoyed this book or found it useful, I'd be very grateful if you'd post a short review on Amazon. Your support does make a difference, and I read all the reviews personally so I can get your feedback and make this book even better.

Thanks again for your support!

www.ingramcontent.com/pod-product-compliance
Lightning Source LLC
Chambersburg PA
CBHW070515160726
48003CB00004B/1581